THE

FORNEY FAMILY

Of Hanover,

PENNSYLVANIA.

———

1690 - 1893.

By

Lucy Forney Bittinger.

Janaway Publishing, Inc.
Santa Maria, California

The Forney Family of Hanover, Pennsylvania. 1690-1893.

Originally published
Pittsburgh, Pennsylvania
1893

Reprinted by:

Janaway Publishing, Inc.
732 Kelsey Ct.
Santa Maria, California 93454
(805) 925-1038
www.JanawayGenealogy.com

2013

ISBN: 978-1-59641-305-4

THE

FORNEY FAMILY

Of Hanover,

PENNSYLVANIA.

1690-1893.

By

Lucy Forney Bittinger.

PUBLISHED FOR MEMBERS OF THE FAMILY.

PITTSBURGH, PA.
PRESS OF SHAW BROTHERS,
1893.

To My Mother,

CATHARINE FORNEY BITTINGER,

THIS RECORD OF HER FAMILY

IS DEDICATED

BY

HER LOVING DAUGHTER.

PREFACE.

The authorities used in the preparation of this record of the descendants of Johann Adam Forney are the Bible and certificate brought with him by the emigrant, the records of churches in Hanover, Pa. and its vicinity, with the baptismal record kept by Jacob Lischy; deeds and wills in the courthouse at York; numerous records from family Bibles; letters from members of the different branches of the family; and inscriptions on tombstones at Hanover.

It may be worth while to state that careful research has failed to show any truth in the tradition—universal among ignorant genealogists—of the "three brothers" who emigrated here, one of whom is said to have settled in Lancaster County and become the ancestor of the late John W. Forney, the second to have gone to North Carolina, and the third to have been Johann Adam Forney.

In regard to the residences of persons mentioned in this history, where no State is mentioned, Pennsylvania may be understood; where no other residence, Hanover.

I shall be very thankful to receive any further information or corrections of this history.

LUCY FORNEY BITTINGER.

SEWICKLEY, PENNSYLVANIA,
    December 2, 1893.

Chapter I.

DESCENDANTS OF

JOHANN ADAM FORNEY, MARX FORNEY, SON OF JOHANN ADAM FORNEY,

AND MARIA EVA (FORNEY) GELWICKS, DAUGHTER

OF MARX FORNEY.

I. THE FORNEY GENEALOGICAL RECORDS,

1690—1893.

JOHANN ADAM FORNEY, born 1690 (?), died 1752 (?), married January, 1713, ELISABETHA LOWISA ——.

MARX, born October 6, 1713, died 1800, married February 16, 1745, BARBEL ——.

- MARIA EVA, born May 26, 1746.
- CHRISTIAN GEORG, born March 26, 1749.
- MARIA CATARINA, born May 3, 1752.
- ANNA MARGARETHA, born May 11, 1755.
- JOHANN ADAM, born February 15, 1757.
- MARX, born April 6, 1760.
- DANIEL, born August 17, 1762.

NICOLAUS, born July 1, 1715, died 1774 (?), married MARIA MAGDALENA ——.

- SOPHIA, married —— MEYER.
  - Anna Margarethe, baptized May 31, 1762.
- JOHANN ADAM, married BARBARA ——.
  - Maria Margarethe, baptized May 31, 1762.
  - Abraham, baptized June 19, 1765.
  - Johann Adam, baptized October 12, 1766.
  - Anna Maria, born July 28, 1773.
  - Anna Catarina, born March 20, 1778.
- HEINRICH, married MAGDALENA ——.
  - Johann Ludwig, baptized Nov. 9, 1766.
  - Johann Peter, born April 20, 1776.
- ABRAHAM, married SUSANNA ——.
  - Maria Magdalena, born June 19, 1774.
- MARGARETHE, married HEINRICH BAYER.
  - Johann Nicolaus, born December 11, 1775.
- PHILIP.
- LEWIS.
- ESTHER.
- JOHANN NICOLAUS.

LOWISA CHARLOTTE, born April 24, 1718, married March 11, 1742, ABRAHAM SELL.

MARIA EVA, born January 6, 1721. (No records.)

PHILIP, born September 29, 1724, died February 3, 1793, married May 8, 1753, ELISABETH SHERZ, born 1732, died August 8, 1794.

- ADAM, born June 15, 1754.
- MARIA, born September 17, 1755.
- LOVICE, born April 26, 1757.
- ELIZABETH, born October 4, 1758.
- PHILIP, born July 7, 1760.
- SAMUEL, born April 23, 1762.
- DAVID, born November 7, 1764.
- PETER, born October 20, 1765.
- HANNAH, born March 27, 1767.
- JACOB, born October 12, 1770.
- SUSANNA, born October 5, 1773.
- SALOME, born February 20, 1776.

CLORA, born February 16, 1728. (No records.)

OUR ancestor, Johann Adam Forney, came to America from Wachenheim-in-the-Haardt, a small town ten miles west of Mannheim. The Haardt is a "splendid tract of country," a mountainous winegrowing district of the Rhenish Palatinate. Cooper, the scene of whose novel, "The Heidenmauer," is laid here, says: "A line of mountains resembling the smaller spurs of the Alleghenies, and which are known by different local names, but which are a branch of the Vosges, passes nearly through the center of the district, in a north and south course. These mountains cease abruptly at their eastern side, leaving between them and the river a vast level surface of that description which is called "flats," or "bottomland," in America. The eastern face of the mountains, or that next the plain, is sufficiently broken and irregular to be beautiful, while it is always distinctly marked and definite. * * * The plain of the Palatinate, far as the eye could reach, lay in the view. Here and there the Rhine and the Neckar glittered like sheets of silver among the verdure of the fields, and tower of city and town, of Mannheim, Spires and Worms, of nameless villages, and of German residences were as plenty in the scene as tombs upon the Appian Way. A dozen gray ruins clung against the sides of the mountains of Baden and Darmstadt, while the castle of Heidelberg was visible in its romantic glen, sombre, courtly and magnificent. The landscape was the perfection of fertility and industry, embellished by a crowd of useful objects."

The family name, which has been spelled Fourny, Fornich, Forny, Farney, Ffarney, Furney, Forne or Forné, Faurney and Farny, is probably French: it is not uncommon in France and French Switzerland. A family tradition says that the Forneys were originally Huguenot refugees from France, who sought an asylum in Germany from religious persecution. Christian Forney, the emigrant's father, had lived in Wachenheim long enough to become a citizen, and they had relatives in the neighboring city of Duerkheim, where representatives of the family still reside. Tradition also tells us of a beautiful daughter of the family, who won the heart of a German nobleman and became his wife. But we must leave tradition for records.

Johann Adam Forney brought with him to this country a certificate, of which the following is a translation; the original is still in the possession of his descendants in Hanover, Pennsylvania:

"We, magistrates, burgomasters and council of the city of Wachenheim-in-the-Haardt, certify herewith that before us came the worthy Johann Adam Forney, citizen and tailor here, the legitimate son of the worthy Christian Forney, also a citizen here, and informed us that he, with his wedded wife, Elisabetha Lowisa, have firmly resolved to set out with their four children and effects, on the journey to the island of Pennsylvania and

* There is in Paris a " Bibliotheque Forney," founded by Samuel Aimé Forney, a Genevan merchant who died in Paris in 1878.

2

to settle there; but he stands in need of an attested certificate of how he behaved with us and why he departed, such as he can show at the place of his settlement. Which we gave him according to his reasonable desire and truthfully; moreover because we believed it would really be required in order that no one could calumniate our citizen or citizen's children; although we have indeed sought diligently and earnestly to dissuade him from such departure, yet he remains of his first intention; therefore after steadfast perseverance we have given the said Johann Adam Forney this certificate: That as long as we have known him he has behaved himself honorably, piously and honestly, as well becomes a good citizen and artisan, and, moreover, showed himself so neighborly that no one has had any complaint to make of him; he also is bound to no compulsory service or serfdom; he will not be unwilling to give, to show with all readiness to those of his intended residence all affection and kindness.

"To this true certificate, we, the authorities, have affixed our city council's great seal to this statement which is given at Wachenheim-in the-Haardt, the 7th of May, 1721."

In his family Bible the emigrant made this record: "In the year 1721, on Oct. 16th, I, Johann Adam Farny and Lowisa Farnisin, with four children, arrived at Philadelphia, in Pennsylvania."

Where they went after landing we do not know. John Digges' bond, dated October 5th, 1731, "to give at some future time an absolute title to the land" which he sold the emigrant, described our ancestor as "Adam Faurney of Philadelphia county, in the Province of Pennsylvania, farmer and tailor," so that he probably spent his first years in America in that county.

He was settled in the neighborhood of what is now Hanover, York county, Pa., in 1734. It was then known as the "Conewago Settlements," or "Digges' Choice." The latter name it got from John Digges, who some years before had taken up some land there on a Maryland warrant, had it surveyed for him by a Maryland surveyor, and had sold some of it to Forney and others, whose lives were "made miserable for years by the turmoils arising out of disputes between Digges and other settlers, which were aggravated by the conflicting claims of Penn and Baltimore to the proprietorship. For many years the region was known as the 'disputed land,' and there was naturally much lawlessness."— [The Hon. Edward McPherson in Gettysburg Star and Sentinel, 1876.]

Adam Forney, in a deposition of August 29, 1746,* gives this account of his dealings with Digges: "That sundry Germans, together with the deponent, having agreed for the purchase of some lands from John Digges, lying at Conewago, after some time, finding that Mr. Digges' claim was of great extent, and did not appear at all ascertained, were solicitous about their deeds and the validity of Mr. Digges' title, and applied to him to that purpose several times and received different accounts from him. At first he told this deponent he had 14,000 acres in the tract, at another time 11,000, and at another time 10,000. This made this deponent and the other settlers still more uneasy and persisting in having his title cleared up. He told this deponent and others he might go to the office at Annapolis and there might see his right and have his lines run, if they would

_____

*Pennsylvania Archives, 1st Series, Vol. II, p. 625, and following.

3

be at the expense of it. That upon this they sent Martin Ungefare to Annapolis, who obtained a copy of the course of his tract from his patent, which contained only 6,822 acres, more or less; that this deponent and others of the settlers then applied to Mr. Thomas Beatty, a magistrate in Prince George's county, to run the lines in order to have them marked, which Mr. Digges opposed, and gathered a body of people to hinder him, and when all his efforts were insufficient to hinder him he threatened to sue him. That on running these lines it appeared that Mr. Digges claimed a great deal more land than he had a right to by his patent, and that he had even sold or received the consideration money, or security for it, for some lands out of his survey. That upon this Mr. Digges appeared much disturbed, and, as this deponent was informed, made his application to Philadelphia to take up as much of the proprietors' land as would make his tract square and enable him to fulfill his contracts with the people, and afterwards told this deponent that he had been with the Secretary of the province of Pennsylvania, and that he had agreed to let him have the lands adjoining his tract to make it square. But Mr. Cookson coming up soon after and acquainting this deponent and others in the settlement that Mr. Digges' application was not effectual, and any of the settlers without his tract that should apply to the land office for warrants upon the common terms might be admitted to have them; this put Mr. Digges, as this deponent apprehends, upon his extraordinary method of a warrant of resurvey which Mr. Digges pretends to have obtained from the land office at Annapolis, under pretext of which he has not only surveyed in those tracts which had fallen out of his original survey, and for which he had contracted for the sale, but also several others, some of which were possessed by virtue of a warrant and surveys from the land office of Pennsylvania and part of some tracts which were patented, particularly about 60 acres of this deponent's."

Thomas Cookson, surveyor of Lancaster county, was sent by the Pennsylvania authorities to read the Royal Order to Digges in the spring of 1746. This Royal Order was designed to settle the vexed question of the boundary between the provinces, and in this case it bore upon Digges' right to take up vacant land in Pennsylvania on his Maryland warrant. But this invocation of the majesty of the law was without effect, as we see from the following letter with its quaint German idioms, from "Adam Forne to Thomas Cookson:"

"Worshipful Sir:

"May it please your worship we cannot but acquaint your worship what has happened here since your departure from us. Yesterday as the 24th of April, Mr. Digges sent a Deputy Sheriff out of Maryland for to arrest Matthew Ulrich and Nicholas Forne he took them two until to my house where I asked the Sheriff by what authority he rested those men, if they owed any money. If they owed money I would be bound for their appearance at Court, but if he could not tell me no more cause as this, viz.: 'that those men should give their bonds to Digges for the land or depart from the land.' The two people have taken up their lands these five years ago from the Hon'r Propr's land office in Philadelphia and it was Surveyed for the same. I ordered upon this them two men as Matthias Ulrich and Nicholas Forne to return to their Habitation, whereupon the Sheriff and Digges' Son made resistance and the Sheriff drew his sword upon me and we then

4

drew our swords and was a-going in upon them, whereupon they fled to their horses and so ran away and so was the way that we got ridden of our new guests. Now is our Humble request to you for to come up Speedily and to look into the matter and settle it that we may have rest and live in peace and quietness as his Majesty's Subjects and not be troubled forever. For if this matter is not rectified and we do not get help speedily we must help ourselves and should it be with our last Drop of Blood, for I am well assured that we will not be put upon by no Digges that ever lived under the Sun. So wishing that you may soon come over, I have no more to add but Remain your

"Humble & Ob't Servant

"Little Canowako,   ADAM FORNE.
    "April 25, 1746."

    "P. S. Sir:—Digges also troubled many more—in short all them that lives in his resurveyed additional lines and was going to have them arrested, but some sent him a-packing in the striving, and yesterday I heard that he should have said that he had made up with your Worship, and if you did not come in Ten days you would not come in Ten years any more."

Apparently the Maryland officers stayed away from the "Disputed Land," after these vigorous measures, and we hear nothing more of the Digges affair until, in January of 1747, the following petition from the inhabitants of Conewago was received:

"Mr. Cookson, these cooms to acquaint you of the yuseige we met with of Mr. Digges and of the government of Maryland. Last week came an officer from Maryland to serve an writ on Adam Forney at the suite of Mr. Jno. Digges of an Trispess on the Case, which officer come to the house of Adam Furney with two negro men and one convict sarvant fallo of said Jno. Digges with Three men more of little better reputation, as we are informed, and as soon as the said persons intred the house they fall upon Adam Furney, draged him out like a Dog, never gave him lave to put on any close but what he had on and so hoisted him away thro a bitter cold night. When Adam Furney's Wife and Daughter under a grate fright and seprise seeing the old man so barbarously used, fell about the old man not knowing what was the matter lamenting and crying, when this convict fallow up with an grate Club Knockt down both the women and so followed up his blows and knockt the Old Woman twice more after they had the old man out as if he had been ordered to commit murder or some other outragies mischief. And that all without any Resin as none of us ever took up Either hand Stick or any other thing, to hurt any of them or to ower defence."

Adam Forney's deposition, taken in Philadelphia, confirms this account: "On the 26th day of January last past this deponent being at his Dwelling House and Plantation situated on Little Conewago about nine miles (as this deponent understands and believes) within and on the Pennsylvania side of the Line commonly called the Temporary Line between the provinces of Pennsylvania and Maryland. He, the said deponent, was then and there arrested by one John Wilmot who called himself the under Sheriff of Baltimore County in Maryland, at the suit of Mr. John Digges, and the said Wilmot having brought with him six other men all with large clubs in their hands, they laid violent hands on this deponent, forced him out of his Dwelling House and carried him away a prisoner down to Baltimore Town in Maryland, and there this deponent entering Bail to the suit thereby obtained his Liberty. And this Deponent saith that before the said Wilmot and his Company took this Deponent out of his house as aforesaid, some of them struck Louisa, this Deponent's wife and Eve his Daughter several violent blows with their said Clubs and gave his said Daughter a deep wound in the Head."

Next comes a letter from R. Peters to Cookson in which he says: "I am obliged to tell you that the whole will turn on this single point whether the place where Adam Farney was arrested be or be not within our Province."

Cookson replies: "Yesterday some people came down from Adam Furne in order to go to Philadelphia for directions how they Should act at the Supreme court at Annapolis. They are Clear intelligible people and speak English Well. I find by them that the point in which you expected it to turn in our favor is against us; the spot where Adam Furney and his son were arrested is actually within Digges' Old Survey and Patent Land. This I have repeatedly asked them and find them as positive and Certain that it is so. From this you cannot Expect to have your action dismissed, but upon the merits that the place in which the Trespass is supposed to be done is within the province of Pennsylvania."

On this Peters wrote to the Maryland attorney who had been retained by the Pennsylvania authorities to defend Forney: "I have just now received a letter from Mr. Cookson who has had the Examination of some sensible people in Furney's neighborhood and they tell him that the place where Furney was arrested is actually within Mr. Digges' Tract, and if so it is no affair of our Province and therefore I have the Governor's orders to send a special messenger to you to prevent you being concerned for or anyways appearing on behalf of our Proprietors or of this Province. Let Adam Furney defend his own cause, since he has entirely misrepresented the situation of the place where he was arrested. * * * But though you are not to appear on behalf of this Government yet if Adam Furney applies to you, I don't mean to hurt the man though I have just reason to be angry with him. I look upon him to be egregiously abused and that Digges has sold him land which belongs to our Proprietors and that if his case were well understood Digges could never recover one Farthing against him, but this is his own concern and of a private nature."

And to Adam Forney he wrote: "I asked you over and over whether your House was within or without of the lines of Digges' Tract, and you not only told me but I think took your Oath that it was at some distance from that tract within our Province and upon this information which you said could be supported by all the neighborhood I have been at the trouble of writing to Mr. Calder to appear for you and did propose to have given him a proper fee but now that I have received better information of Mr. Cookson that the place where you was arrested is within Mr. Digges' patented lines, I have withdrawn my retainer of Mr. Calder and you are now left to make your own defence in the best manner you can. Do not mistake me as if I meant to say by this that Mr. Digges has any right to an inch of ground but what is within his Lines and if you pay him for any Land out of his Lines you pay in your own wrong and our Proprietors if they have not been already paid will be paid again for that very land and if at Mr. Digges' Suit a Maryland Sheriff serves a writ on any land out of his patented lines he will be guilty of a breach of the Royal Order and will then do an injury to this government which will be properly treated. But your case is of a nature that no ways concerns our Proprietors though I owe to you that it would be no difficult matter for you to put Mr. Digges in the wrong if you had an able Lawyer and could make it appear that he has sold you Land that does not belong to him.

"I am on all proper occasions,

"Your Friend to serve you,

"R. PETERS."

It does not appear, however, that Forney was asked at first whether his house was on land which had at any time been claimed by Digges, only whether his home was North of the "Temporary Line" separating the provinces of Maryland and Pennsylvania; neither was it within Digges' "old survey" of 1732. It was on his "resurvey" in 1745 that he took it in, and this resurvey was thought to be unauthorized and fraudulent, both by the inhabitants of Conewago and by the Proprietors of Pennsylvania. The matter, however, is very confused and complicated, and at this distance of time nearly unintelligible, and Adam Forney may be readily excused if he made a misstatement in the matter. It is not known how his case ended.

The pioneer's life seems to have been a troublous one. In 1748 we find noted in the minutes of the Provincial Council that "An Indian this last summer came in a rude manner to a substantial housekeeper of Lancaster county, one Adam Furney and demanded rum of him; he gave him some; but because he refused to give him more he withdrew a small space, and having his gun in his hand ready loaded he shot him in the breast, and he lay a considerable time ill of his wounds, being expected to die every day. On this the Indian was apprehended and committed to jail, but the man recovered, contrary to all expectations, and the Indian was the other day released."—[Colonial Records, Vol. V, page 409.]

Adam Forney died, probably in the early part of 1752; family tradition says, from the consequences of the wound inflicted by the Indian. His wife survived him at least a year, for on July 20, 1753, she filed her account as administratrix of her husband's estate, which was appraised at £1021 13s 9d.

Johann Adam Forney and Lowisa Elizabetha his wife had six children: Marx, Nicolaus, Lowisa Charlotte, Maria Eva, Philip and Clora.

CHILDREN OF MARX FORNEY AND HIS WIFE.

JOHANN ADAM FORNEY AND ELISABETHA LOWISA

MARX FORNEY, born October 6, 1713, died 1800, married February 16, 1745, BARBEL.

MARIA EVA, born May 25, 1746, died 1789(?), married July 2, 1765, CALL GENWICKS, born September 16, 1741.

EVE CATHARINE, born Mar. 29, 1756, died February 1, 1841, married CHRISTIAN WIRT, born May 12, 1763, died March 2, 1842.

Maria, born September 19, 1757, died August 28, 1805, married 1806, Jacob Eichelberger, born April 24, 1775, died August 18, 1843.

Matthew, born October 27, 1807, died 1883, married Sarah (Tucker) Ickes.

- Mary Kate, married H. De Armau.
  - Estelle. Jesse. Storti. Rufus. Bessie. Maggie.
- Elizabeth, married Jesse Garrett.
- Sarah F., married C. L. Cunningham.
  - Willie. Katie. George E. Louis. Abdiel Wirt. Charles. Mary.

Jacob, born August 28, 1811, died November 4, 1881, married, 1st, Asenath Scoggin.

- Maria (died in childhood.)
- Charley, married, 1st, N. Brooks,
  - Stella. Pauline. Wirt. Yessie. Maud. Maggie. Kate. Charles.
- 2d, Emma Taylor.
- Anna M., married H. R. Mullins, M. D.
  - Maud. Kate. Lemuel.
- Jacob, M. D.
- Charles.
- Ora A., married R. F. Forrester.
  - Maggie.
- Catharine, married J. N. Sudduth.
  - Estella. John L.
- Mary, married Thomas Holly.
- Ida, married Gluer Trent.
  - Carrie Belle, married Wm. White.
  - Thomas C. Mattie. Kate. Amelia. George L. Charles Wirt.
- Abdiel W.
- Newton C. George F. Mary Kate.
- Martha, married George L. Cunningham.
- Jacob (died in youth.)

Married 2d, Charlotte (Stewart) Allen.

- George W., married Emma French Allen.
  - Paul Metzgar. Ray. Jacob. George. Sallie.

Henry, born October 27, 1818, died February 28, 1890.

8

JOHANN ADAM FORNEY AND ELISABETHA LOWISA ——

MARX FORNEY AND BARBEL ——

MARIA EVA FORNEY AND GEORG CARL GELWICKS

EVA CATHARINE GELWICKS AND CHRISTIAN WIRT.

Maria Wirt and Jacob Eichelberger.

Catharine Matilda, born May 4, 1817, died September 8, 1868, married Samuel Alexander McCosh.
- Mary, married Nathan Baker.
  - Mary Louisa.
  - James Henry.
  - Cornelius Edwin.
  - Silas Whittier.
- James, married Mary Elizabeth Birdsong.
  - Abdiel Samuel.
  - Anna Rebecca.
  - John Birdsong.
  - Ruth.
- Louisa, married James Hines.
  - Nancy Catharine, married John L. Hill, M. P.
  - Cornelius Elmer.
  - James Alexander.
  - Sarah Louisa.
  - Annie Dixon.
  - Mary Wirt.
  - Hugh (died in infancy.)
- Samuel A. died May 1880, married Louisa Kellogg.
  - Nathaniel.
  - Rufus Eichelberger.
  - Marshall.
  - Alice Louisa.
- Cornelius R., married Nancy Baugher.
  - Irene.
  - Hy. Eichelberger.
  - Robert.
  - Louisa.
- Henry Clay (died in infancy.)
- Catharine Matilda, married Jas. Ware.
  - Samuel Alexander.
  - Melvin.
  - Matthew.
  - Cornelius.

Abdiel Wirt.

Rufus, born May 20, 1822, died August 3, 1885.
- Mary, married Paul Hersh.

Amanda, born September 14, 1825, died May 2, 1871, married Abdiel F. Gitt.
- Kate, married William Himes.
  - Anna.
  - Amelia Eichelberger.
  - Helen.
  - William.

Amelia Henrietta.

Louisa Anna, born February 14, 1816, died ——, married William Johnston.
- Catharine Mary.
- William.
- Octd, died ——
- Martha Jane.

Henry, born October 9, 1789, died April 14, 1862, married March 9, 1815, Catharine Swope, born May 16, 1796, died April 19, 1876.

Catharine, born November 11, 1817, died August 24, 1873, married Andrew Keyser.
- Henry Wirt, married Mary Winebrenner.
- Frederick Austin, died.
- Eliza Reveile, married David Edwin Winebrenner.
- Anna Kate.
- Louis Edwin.
- Helen Josephine, (died in infancy.)

William Edwin, born December 14, 1819, died ——

Rebecca, born October 9, 1821, died July 28, 1896, married Joseph Eichelberger Cremer.
- Mary, died.
- Kate.

Ann Maria, born August 25, 1823, died August 22, 1854, married George Eichelberger.
- Henry Wirt, born January 8, 1844 died November 7, 1891.
- Chas. Edwin, born September 10, 1847, died December 8, 1888.
- Blanche, married Samuel Schmucker Sneltzer.

9

CHILDREN OF MARX FORNEY AND HIS WIFE—CONTINUED.

JOHANN ADAM FORNEY AND ELISABETHA LOWISA

MARX FORNEY AND BARBEL

Henry Wirt and Catharine Swope.

Ellen, born March 30, 1825, died July 10, 1884, married John Willy Crapster O'Neal.

- Catharine E.
- Walter Henry, married Martha Hay.
  - Hay Wirt (died in infancy.)
  - Ellen.
  - Alexander Hay.
- John Willy (died in infancy.)
- Mary Ellen, married John Crapster.
  - Ellen Patterson.
  - Lucy (died in infancy.)
  - Anna.
  - Christine Wirt (died in infancy.)
  - John O'Neal.
- Anna Wirt.
- Elmira Virginia.

Henry, born February 23, 1827, died December 9, 1860, married Louisa Elizabeth Forney.

Sarah, born January 8, 1829, died March 5, 1844, married Louis Eichelberger.

William Wirt.

Emaline, born September 5, 1833, died October 27, 1834.

EVE CATHARINE GELWICKS AND CHRISTIAN WIRT.

Catharine, born March 1, 1792, died April 20, 1842, married George Emmert, born September 4, 1789, died April 16, 1841.

Horatio Wirt, born March 12, 1812, died August 13, 1867, married Susan R. Gitt, died February 8, 1863.

- Adalin Catharine, died April 12, 1860.
- Mary Elizabeth, died December 20, 1854.
- Valeria Delilah, married Augustus McFarland.
  - Irma, died.
  - Alveria.
- Olivia Susan, died December 26, 1850.
- Mary Alveria, died November 8, 1855.
- Laura Virginia, married George Marks.
  - Lottie, died.
  - Raymond.
- Lawson, married Bertha Snyder.
  - Maria.
  - Susanna.
  - Edward.

Martha Susan, died January 11, 1859.

Catharine, born April 24, 1814, died March 28, 1846.
Delilah Matilda, born July 16, 1818, died January 28, 1842.

Franklin Guncle, born September 28, 1820, married Jane Bowers.
- Annie.
- Michael.
- Horatio.
- Sadie.

George Wellington, born November 23, 1822, died March 19, 1860.
Washington, born March 1, 1824, died June 1, 1846.
Augustus, born May 1, 1827, died September 17, 1845.

William, born March 29, 1829, died July 4, 1893, married Sarah Schwartz.
- George.
- Gilbert.
- Charles.
- Katie.
- William.

Henry, born March 30, 1831, died November 12, 1847.
Ann Maria, born December 16, 1883, died January 25, 1851.

Lydia, born February 1, 1738, married Adam Forney. (See records.)

10

CHILDREN OF MARX FORNEY AND HIS WIFE—CONTINUED.

JOHANN ADAM FORNEY AND ELISABETHA LOWISA ——

MARX FORNEY AND BARDEL ——

MARIA EVA FORNEY AND GEORG CARL GELWICKS

EVE CATHARINE GELWICKS AND CHRISTIAN WIRT.

Jacob, born February 24, 1801, died November 8, 1869, married November 20, 1827, Amelia Danner.

Emma Catharine, born May 28, 1829, died 1862, married John A. Swope.

Ella, married 1st, —— Helmel, 2d, —— Daily, 3d, —— Curler. { Norman. | John Swope, died 1891.

Margaret, married James L. A. Burrell, M. D., died October, 1891. { James. Blanche M. John Swope.

Emma. (died in infancy.) Catharine, married Harry Claybaugh. { Helen. Emma C.

Alexander Christian, born November 13, 1831, died January 24, 1884.

Jacob, born February 29, 1834, died March 20, 1842.

Eliza Ann, born May 10, 1836, married George S. Forney. (See records.)

Martha, born August 26, 1838, married Albert McClean Barnitz. { Jacob Percival, married Mary Barnitz. Wirt Whitcomb. Anna, died. Richard. Emma Wirt.

Danner, born October 21, 1840, died September 1, 1841.

Ruel, born July 20, 1842, died June 8, 1845.

Calvin Clay, born April 12, 1844, died February 4, 1871, married Ellen Buehler.

Florence Amelia, born March 29, 1846, died July 6, 1846.

Robert Millard, born January 16, 1854, married June 29, 1875, Bertha Barnitz. { Amelia Danner, born June 28, 1876. Charles Barnitz, born April 16, 1878. Robert Oglesby, born April 18, 1880.

William, born June 21, 1804, died June 15, 1875, married first, Anna Blitz.

Married 2d, Catharine (Blitz) Forrest.

Emory, born 1837, died November 11, 1864, married Emma Jane Schriver. { Carrie A. (died in infancy.) William H. (died in infancy.) Katharine, married Harry Wilcox.

Thomas, married Catharine Kohler. { Laura. William. Sadie. Bertha.

Hester A., born 1844, died December 8, 1870.

Catharine, born 1847, died March 6, 1866.

Jane Edith, born 1851, died February 25, 1852.

Delilah Adelia, born July 20, 1807, died June 24, 1887, married George W. Hinkle, born August 26, 1804, died November 30, 1866.

George W., born August 7, 1827, died April 27, 1844.

Catharine Jane, born October 8, 1832, died July 17, 1850, married June 3, 1851, Matthias Eichelberger Trone. { Emily.

11

MARX FORNEY, the eldest son of the emigrant Johann Adam, was born in Wachenheim, "and his sponsor was the worthy Marx Oberle." He was brought to Pennsylvania by his parents when eight years old; he was probably brought up in Philadelphia county, but in 1734, when we find the family at the "Conewago settlements," he was of age. His wife's name cannot be deciphered with certainty, but was probably "Barbel," or Barbara. Her family name we do not know. In 1750, when York county was set off from Lancaster, "Marks Forney" was the first supervisor of Manheim Township. Three years later he was naturalized, a step rarely taken save by those who had considerable connection with the outside English world. Mr. Samuel H. Forney has an old account book with the name "Johann Adam Farne," and the date 1741, also Marx's name and the same date: it proves that one or both of them kept tavern at the homestead. Later, Marx moved on to the land now owned by Mr. Abner W. Forney, where he built a log house in the north corner of the present door-yard; the well still remains. Over a spring a short distance away, he erected a stone spring-house, with a stone over the door, inscribed "1760. Marx Farny." This stone is in possession of Mr. David F. Forney. Tradition says that Marx was wealthy, a statement borne out by his will, dated April 30, 1800. By it he left either a farm or a house to each of his four sons, and £400 to be divided between his daughter and grand-daughter; his wife, apparently, died before him.

The children of Marx Forney and his wife were Maria Eva, Christian Georg, Maria Catarina, Anna Margaretha, Johann Adam, Marx and Daniel.

MARIA EVA FORNEY married Georg Carl Gelwicks. He was a member of a family then prominent in Hanover, and was an innkeeper. On November 3, 1775, he was chosen on the Committee of Conference for York county, and on March 30, 1776, we have a communication from him and others relating to the unpatriotic utterances of a certain Robert Owings, from whom they demanded and received the declaration of his repentance. In 1778 he was in the militia of York county, being lieutenant of the Second company of the Eighth batallion. His wife, Eva, died young, leaving one child, Eve Catharine.

Concerning EVE CATHARINE GELWICKS, this rather romantic tradition has been preserved by Mr. Henry Wirt, in his notebook: "Michael Fisher tells me that he used to hear his aunts say that Grandmother Wirt, whose maiden name was Gelwicks, was a daughter of one of the daughters of Marx Forney, who intermarried with a Mr. Gelwicks. Grandmother's mother died when she was yet a child, and her father marrying again, she was driven out by her stepmother and had quite a hard time. At the death of Marx Forney, she is said to have inherited a large sum, the tradition being that Marx, who was considered a very wealthy man, had a chest full of silver, which all went to Grandmother, and the sons took the land." She married Christian, son of Henry Wirt, who emigrated in 1738 and married Mrs. Anna Jaeger, the widow of his employer; they lived on a farm near Iron Ridge. Christian Wirt was a saddler by trade, but later opened a store in the old building at the corner of Baltimore street and the public square in Hanover, now occupied by Wentz & Overbaugh. In this mercantile enterprise he made what was regarded in those days as a large fortune.

Christian and Eve (Gelwicks) Wirt had seven children: Maria, Henry, Catharine, Lydia, Jacob, William and Deliah Adella.

MARIA WIRT was the second wife of Jacob Eichelberger, who was "a merchant and farmer, and kept a public house, which was long known as the 'Stage Office,' now the Central Hotel. He was the first president of the Maryland Line Turnpike Company, and was also the president of the Hanover Savings Fund Society for a number of years."

The children of Jacob and Maria (Wirt) Eichelberger are Matthew, Jacob, Henry, Catharine Matilda, Abdiel Wirt, Rufus A., Amanda and Amelia Henrietta.

MATTHEW EICHELBERGER at one time conducted an extensive store business at Abbottstown, but for over thirty years lived at Gettysburg, retired from active business. He was married to Mrs. Sarah (Tucker) Ickes; he had no children.

JACOB EICHELBERGER resided in Alabama, where he owned and operated the Wehadkee flour and sawmills; he was married, first, to Asenath Scoggins, and secondly, to Mrs. Charlotte (Stewart) Allen and had eight children: Elizabeth, Maria, Charles, Catharine, Mary, Martha, Jacob and George.

HENRY EICHELBERGER resided in earlier life in Abbottstown, engaged in tanning; he afterwards returned to Hanover and was a farmer; he never married.

CATHARINE MATILDA EICHELBERGER married Samuel Alexander McCosh, who probably died in the Confederate service; he was in a hospital which was burnt, and was never heard of afterwards. She resided in Georgia and died there, leaving a family of seven children: Mary, James, Louisa, Samuel, Cornelius, Henry Clay and Catharine Matilda.

ABDIEL WIRT EICHELBERGER, universally known as "The Captain," was brought up in Hanover. When a young man he joined his brother Jacob in Georgia. "Whilst there he arranged for the shipment of carriages and of damask coverlets to that State, which business he continued for several years, and subsequently purchased, with his brother, the Wehadkee mills, and has since held his interest in the same, except during the Civil War, when the property was confiscated by the Confederate Government, and returned to him after the war. From 1845 to 1852 he spent his winters in the South and his summers in Hanover," devoting some of his spare time to the drilling of a militia company, whence he obtained his title. He was then elected president of the Hanover Branch R. R., and still retains the position nominally, "being in term of continuous service the oldest railroad president in the United States." He is thoroughly informed respecting family history, the quotations above being taken from an article on the Eichelberger family, supplied by him to Gibson's History of York County. He has never married.

RUFUS A. EICHELBERGER was also unmarried. He was for some years president of the Hanover Savings Fund Society. It is an interesting circumstance that the five presidents of this institution, which was founded by M. N. Forney, were all descended from or allied to the emigrant Johann Adam Forney: they are Jacob Eichelberger, Jacob Wirt, Henry Wirt, Rufus Eichelberger, and Robert Wirt.

AMANDA EICHELBERGER was married to Abdiel F. Gitt of New Oxford, where she lived and died, leaving two daughters, Mary and Kate.

AMELIA HENRIETTA EICHELBERGER resides with her brother at Hanover. I am indebted to her for the collection of much of this information.

HENRY WIRT, the oldest son of Christian, succeeded his father in the latter's mercantile business, and, after retiring from active pursuits, "took great interest," says his son, "in all the movements which were then made for the good of the town of Hanover." He was First Lieutenant of the company commanded by Capt. Metzger, which marched to the defense of Baltimore in 1814. He helped to organize the first Sunday School in the town, and also to introduce the common school system there; strange to say, both movements met with determined opposition. He was also interested in the building of the Hanover Branch R. R.

Henry Wirt married Catharine Swope, and they had nine children: Louisa Anna, Catharine, William Edwin, Rebecca, Ann Maria, Ellen, Henry, Sarah and Emeline, who died in infancy.

LOUISA ANNA WIRT married Dr. William Johnston, a physician of York. They had four children: Martha and Kate, now residing in York; Ovid, who died some years since in the West; and William, married, and residing West.

CATHARINE WIRT married Andrew Keyser Shriver of Union Mills, Md., where they resided all their lives. He was a nephew of Rachel Shriver, wife of Adam Forney, and a distant collateral relative of Ludwig Shriver, who married Maria Forney. The children of Andrew Keyser and Catharine (Wirt) Shriver are Henry Wirt, Frederick Austin, Eliza Brengle, Kate, Louis Edwin and Helen Josephine, who died in infancy.

HENRY WIRT SHRIVER occupies the old homestead at "the Mills," and has been engaged in tanning and farming. He was in the Emergency militia during the war. He and his wife, Mary Jane (Winebrenner) Shriver have had five children: Lucy (who died as an infant), Elizabeth, Henry Wirt, Mary Winifred and Sarah Catharine.

FREDERICK AUSTIN SHRIVER was engaged in the tannery with his brothers until ill health compelled him to give up active life; he is now dead.

ELIZA BRENGLE SHRIVER is married to David E. Winebrenner, a brother of Mrs. Wirt Shriver. They live in Hanover, and have three children: Helen Shriver, Martha Catharine and David Edwin.

Miss ANNA KATE SHRIVER also resides in Hanover, while LOUIS EDWIN SHRIVER is in business at the Union Mills.

WILLIAM EDWIN WIRT died in early manhood.

REBECCA WIRT married Joseph Eichelberger Cremer; they had two sons, Henry Wirt and Charles Edwin, both of whom died unmarried, and this family is extinct.

ANN MARIA WIRT was married to George Eichelberger of Charlestown, Va., and died shortly after, leaving one child, Blanche, who was brought up by her grandmother Wirt in Hanover; she married S. S. Smeltzer, a resident, and at one time, mayor of Staunton, Va., where he died in 1891. Of their four children, the two eldest died within a few days of each other, of scarlet fever.

ELLEN WIRT married John Willy Crapster O'Neal, M. D.; they lived for years in Baltimore, then removed to Gettysburg, in which historic town she died, after a lingering illness, of consumption. She had six children: Catharine E., Walter Henry (now practising medicine in Gettysburg), John Willy (who died in infancy), Mary Ellen (married to John Crapster and living near Taneytown, Md.), Anna Wirt and Elmira Virginia.

HENRY WIRT, JR., as he at first signed himself, was the only surviving son of Henry and Catharine (Swope) Wirt. He lived all his life in Hanover, where he was prominent in many business enterprises, notably in the Hanover Branch R. R. and the presidency of the Savings Fund Society. He was very active in the Reformed church, both in his own congregation and the church at large, and was perhaps the most prominent layman in the denomination. He was also a very accurate local antiquary, and much of the information in these pages I owe to his careful researches. He was married to Louisa Elizabeth Forney, daughter of Matthias Nace Forney; they have no children.

SARAH WIRT was married to Louis Eichelberger, M. D., of Charlestown, Va., a brother of Ann Wirt's husband. Mrs. Dr. Eichelberger died at Catonsville, Md., leaving one son, William Wirt, who was employed in the Signal Service of the Government and died in 1886, leaving a widow and five children, two of whom have since died.

CATHARINE WIRT, daughter of Christian, married George Emmert; they lived in Hanover and died there, both in middle life, leaving a large family of children. The daughters, Catherine, Deliah and Ann Maria, kept house for the brothers, most of whom were clerks in the Wirt store, but a number of the family died young and unmarried, of consumption, seven of them thus passing away a few years after their parent's death.

The children of George and Catharine (Wirt) Emmert were Horatio Wirt, Catherine, Deliah Matilda, Franklin Gunckle, George Wellington, Washington, Augustus, William, Henry and Ann Maria. The survivors were Horatio, Franklin and William.

HORATIO WIRT EMMERT, with his brother Wellington, conducted a mercantile business for himself, after William Wirt gave up his. He was married to Susan Gitt; of their eight children—Athalia Catherine, Mary Elizabeth, Valeria Deliah, Olivia Susan, Mary Alverta, Laura Virginia, Lawson and Martha Susan—but three survive. They are Valeria, married to Augustus McFarland, Laura, to George Marks, and Lawson, who married Bertha Snyder and now lives in Pittsburg.

FRANKLIN GUNCKLE EMMERT is married to Jane Bowers and is a farmer, living in the neighborhood of Hanover; he has four children, the three eldest being married.

WILLIAM EMMERT died recently in New Oxford. He was married to Sarah Schwartz, and they have five children: George, Gilbert, Charles, Katie and William.

LYDIA WIRT was married to Adam Forney; to his name the reader will refer.

JACOB WIRT succeeded his brother Henry in the management of the business originally established by their father; subsequently he was the first president of the Hanover Branch R. R. and also of the Savings Fund Society. He was married to Amelia Danner and they had ten children: Emma Catharine, Alexander Christian, Jacob, Eliza Ann, Martha, Danner, Ruel, Calvin Clay, Florence Amelia and Robert Millard. Of these, Alexander, Jacob, Danner, Ruel and Florence died young.

EMMA CATHARINE WIRT was married to Dr. John A. Swope of Gettysburg, where she lived, and died in early womanhood, leaving three daughters—Ella, Katherine and Margaret—all now married.

ELIZA ANN WIRT married George N. Forney and her family history is given under her husband's name.

MARTHA WIRT was married to Albert Maclean Barnitz of York, where she resided during her brief married life, but after her husband's death, she returned to Hanover, where, with her son and daughter, she now resides.

CALVIN CLAY WIRT was one of the "Emergency men" called out in 1863, then engaged in the banking business in Baltimore, but returned to Hanover and died there in his thirtieth year, leaving a widow, *nee* Ellen Buehler, but no children.

ROBERT MILLARD WIRT, now the only male representative of the Wirt family in Hanover, is the president of the Savings Fund Society and is interested in various other business enterprises of the town. He and his wife (formerly Bertha Barnitz, of Middletown, O.) have three children—Aimee, Charles and Robert.

WILLIAM WIRT, youngest son of Christian, was also engaged for a time in the family store. He was an ardent Methodist. He and his first wife, Anna Ritz, had five children: Emory, Thomas, Hester A., Catherine and Jane Edith, who died in infancy. The other daughters also died young, as did Emory, who left a widow, *nee* Emma Schriver, since re-married; he was survived by one child, Katherine. The second son, Thomas, now lives in Parsons, Kansas. William Wirt and his second wife, Catharine (Ritz) Forrest, had no children.

DELIAH ADELLA WIRT was the first wife of George W. Hinkle, M. D., of Hanover; she died young, leaving a son, George W., who died in his seventeenth year and a daughter, Catherine Jane, married to Matthias E. Trone; she also died young, leaving but one child, Emily, who has made her home since childhood with her father's sister, Mrs. Daniel Albright of Hanover.

Chapter II.

—

DESCENDANTS OF

CHRISTIAN GEORG FORNEY, MARIA CATARINA (FORNEY) KIEFAUBER,
ANNA MARGARETHA FORNEY, JOHN ADAM FORNEY,
CHILDREN OF MARX FORNEY, AND GRAND
CHILDREN OF JOHANN ADAM FORNEY.

JOHANN ADAM FORNEY AND ELISABETHA LOWISA ——.

MARX FORNEY AND BARBEL ——.

ELIZABETH, married JACOB BOYER.
- Jacob, married —— Yeagy.
- John, married Julian Gulden.
- Polly, died.
- Rebecca, married, 1st, —— Yeagy; 2d, —— Gels.
- Elizabeth, married William Kiefauver.
- Susanna, died.
- Annie, married Samuel Delap.

JOHN DANIEL, married SUSANNA MILLER.
- Adam, married —— Gulden.
- Eliza, died.
- Mary, married, 1st, Henry Sheely; 2d, —— Hauptmann.
- Daniel.
- Sally, married George Hoffman.
- Susanna, married William Haugh.
- James.
- Samuel.
- Malinda, married —— Hoffman.

CHRISTIAN GEORG FORNEY, born Mar. 26, 1749, died August 11, 1824, married, 1st,

JOHN CHRISTIAN, born January 21, 1795, died April 14, 1870, married ELIZABETH LARICH, born January 17, 1799, died March 31, 1881.
- Lydia, married Adam Sowers.
- Jacob.
- Eliza, married Henry Mummert.
- Maria, married Samuel Shaeffer.
- Mandilla, married Henry Mayer.
- Sarah, married David Rabenstine.
- Susanna, married Jesse Shorb.
- Catharine, married Charles Blocher.
- Polly, married Henry Kaltrider.
- Louisa, married Leander Frock.

JACOB, born February 1, 1797, died January 5, 1872, married, 1st, CATHARINE MILLER, born February 15, 1791, died August 28, 1845.
Married, 2d, LYDIA LARICH, born September 6, 1803, died July 18, 1878.
- Lydia, married George Kraft.
- Amanda, married Henry Siegfried.
- Josiah, married Elizabeth Stine.
- Eliza, married Andrew Miller.
- Maria, married —— Rohrbach.
- Jerome, married Elizabeth Trone.
- Ann Caroline, married Jesse Becker.
- Anna Martha, married, 1st, William Rohrbach; 2d, —— Willet.

MATTHIAS, born March 16, 1799, died April 20, 1879, married, 1st, MARIA ELIZABETH ROWERSOX, born 1800 (?), died December, 1846.
- Margaret, married Charles Rontson.
- John Christian, born April 10, 1826, died June 20, 1878.
- Emanuel, born October 15, 1827, married April 21, 1851, Mary Petry, born March 13, 1827.
  - Daniel.
  - Catharine, married Luther Petry.
    - Ora E.
  - Elizabeth, died March 17, 1862.
  - Mary Ann, died February 28, 1862.
  - Sarah, died April 10, 1862.
  - William, married Anna Clark.
    - Hazel Catharine.
  - Anna.
  - Martha Jane.
- William, married Mary Ann Shuss.
- Louisa Anna, died March 27, 1855.
- Elizabeth (died in childhood.)
- Matthias, born March 7, 1839, died 1839.
- Amanda (died in infancy.)
- Mary Ann.

Married, 2d, ——
- Sarah, died April 16, 1869.
- George.
- Christian.
- David.
- Rebecca.
- Jane, died.
- Daniel.

REBECCA, married JOHN MILLER.
- Henry, died, married Margaret Lynch.
- Magdalena (died in infancy.)
- Lydia.
- Elizabeth, died, married Ephraim Graybill.
- Rebecca, married Joseph Utz.
- Ann Maria, married John Lau.
- Louisa, died.
- Catharine, died 1880, married Henry Rabenstine.
- John William, married Mary Herman.

2d, ANNA MARIA MILLER, born June 7, 1769, died March 24, 1845.

MARIA CATARINA FORNEY, born May 3, 1752, married NICOLAUS KIEFAUVER, born September 29, 1751.
- JOHANN NICOLAUS, born July 8, 1773.
- MARIA CATARINA, born October 6, 1775.
- PETER, born 1778.
  - No records.

ANNA MARGARETHA, born May 11, 1755, died February 23, 1775.

CHRISTIAN GEORG FORNEY received from his father Marx, a farm of about 160 acres, one part of which Marx had inherited from his father, Johann Adam, and the other part, bought from the Penns. This farm passed to his sons, who were not able to keep it, and it is now owned by Mrs. S. G. Witmer. Christian Forney's second wife was a widow, Mrs. Miller, who had several children by her first marriage; his first wife's name I do not know.

The children of Christian Forney and his first wife were Elizabeth, John Daniel, John Christian, Jacob, Matthias and Rebecca.

ELIZABETH FORNEY married Jacob Boyer; they lived near Bendersville, Adams Co., and had several children: Jacob, John, Polly (who died unmarried), Rebecca, Elizabeth, Susanna (who also died single), and Anna.

JOHN DANIEL FORNEY married Susanna Miller, a daughter of his step-mother by her first marriage. He lived in Woodsboro', Md., and had nine children: Adam, Eliza, Mary, Daniel, Sally, Susanna, James, Samuel and Melinda. Eliza was drowned when a child by falling into the well on the farm now owned by Jesse Rice. Adam lives at Two Taverns, Adams Co., as does his unmarried brother Daniel.

JOHN CHRISTIAN FORNEY lived in West Manheim Township, on a farm now occupied by Adam Miller; he was married to Elizabeth Larich, and they had ten children: Lydia, Jacob, Eliza, Maria, Mandilla, Sarah, Susanna, Catherine, Polly and Louisa. Lydia married Adam Sowers and moved to the West; Jacob, the only son, a bachelor, lives with his sister Louisa, not far from St. Bartholomew's church, while Susanna and Sarah, both widowed, live in the same neighborhood; Maria and Polly live in Carroll County, Md.; Catherine, now dead, resided near Gitt's Mill, and Mandilla resides near what is known as the "Stone Church," in Wentz's Valley, on the line between Pennsylvania and Maryland.

JACOB FORNEY was commonly called "Bush Jake," or in English, "Farmer Jake," in distinction from another of the same name, Jacob Forney of Hanover, son of Adam and Rachel (Shriver) Forney. "Farmer" Jacob Forney, married a daughter of his step-mother's first marriage, Catharine Miller; she was killed by a stroke of lightning; some silver spoons, hidden in the clock case, were melted by the same stroke. Her husband subsequently married Lydia Larich, a sister of his brother Christian's wife: they had no children. They lived on a farm next that owned by his father, Christian Georg; it is now owned by Jesse Rice.

The children of Jacob and Catharine (Miller) Forney were Lydia, Amanda, Josiah, Eliza, Maria, Jerome, Ann Caroline and Anna Martha. Jerome moved West and is dead, as is also his brother; but most of the daughters live in or near Hanover.

MATTHIAS FORNEY, called "Tice" after the Pennsylvania German fashion, moved to Morrison's Cove, Bedford County; he first married Elizabeth Bowersox, and they had eight children: Margaret, John, Emanuel, William, Louisa, Elizabeth, Matthias and Mary Ann. John, Louisa, Elizabeth and Matthias died in childhood or youth; Margaret (Mrs. Routson), lives in Hanover; Emanuel at Westminster, Md.; Mary Ann in the West, and William at Everett, Bedford County. By his second marriage Matthias Forney's children were: Sarah, George, Christian, David, Rebecca, Jane and Daniel: of these Sarah and Jane are dead.

18

Rebecca (or Peggy) Forney married another of the widow Miller's children, John. They had nine children: Henry. Magdalena, Lydia, Elizabeth, Rebecca, Ann Maria. Louisa, Catherine and John William. Lena died in childhood, and Louisa unmarried; Lydia moved West, but most of the rest live in or near Hanover.

Maria Catarina Forney, daughter of Marx, was married to Nicholas Kiefauber, who lived in the neighborhood of Littlestown; he was the son of Conrad and Anna Margaretha Kiefauber, and a twin brother of Eva Dorothea, married to Col. Henry Slagle, hereafter mentioned. Catarina (Forney) Kiefauber and her husband had at least three children: Johann Nicolaus, Maria Catarina and Peter, but I cannot learn anything farther about them.

Anna Margaretha Forney died in her twentieth year.

JOHANN ADAM FORNEY AND ELISABETHA DOWISA ——.			

MARX FORNEY AND BARBEL ——.

JOHANN ADAM FORNEY, born February 15, 1757, died June 21, 1834, married August 31, 1782, MARIA CHRISTINA HOFFMAN, born December 26, 1762, died June 15, 1830.

CATHARINE, born October 20, 1783, died Mar. 1, 1849, married DAVID NEWMAN.

- **Jesse David**, born November 15, 1800, died February 29, 1880, married, 1st, Catharine Kuhn.
  - Thomas.
  - Charles E.
  - Holliday.
  - Richard B.
  - Matilda C.
  - Calvin S.
- Married, 2d, Charlotte Stair.
  - Charlotte Eva, married Sept. 6, 1893, Clyde S. Payne.
- **Ephraim David**, born November 14, 1803, married Mary Sterner.
  - Adam P.
  - George W.
  - Catharine.
  - Amos R.
- **Ann Maria**, born March 27, 1808, married Peter Sholl.
  - Kate.
- **Margaret**, born August 19, 1810, married Abraham Brough.
  - Harriet.
- **Michael**, born November 22, 1811.
- **Adam Forney**, born July 14, 1814, died ——, married Mary ——.
  - Catharine M.
  - Harry M.
  - William A.
- **James Ross**, born August 20, 1816, married ——.
  - Franklin.
  - James.
  - John.
- **Lydia Ann**, born November 20, 1820, married Alexander Horner.
  - Albert H.
  - Hanson.
  - Lucy.
  - Catharine.
  - Petty.
- **Julian**, born February 25, 1821, married John Brown.
- **John David**, born July 7, 1828, married ——.
  - Nettie.
  - Ella.
  - Jennie.

MARY CHRISTIANA, married ADAM FISHER.

- **Julian**, married Louis Michael.
  - Catharine, married Al. Kohler.
  - Mary, married Joel Henry.
- **Michael**, married Henrietta Stair.
  - Charlotte Elizabeth.
  - Alice Josephine.
  - Martha Marion.
  - Eva, married Jacob Hostetter.
    - Abraham.
    - Gertrude.
    - Stella.
    - Nettie.
    - Jacob.
    - Ruth.
  - Emma, died February 15, 1880, married Geo. Gilt.
    - William.
    - George.
    - Milton, died.
    - Daisy.
    - Emma, died.
  - Kate, married Jacob Grove.
    - Dade.
    - Kate.
    - Henrietta.
    - John.
    - Jacob (died in infancy.)
  - Michael, married Emma Becker.
  - Gertrude, married Luther Weaver.
    - Catharine.
- **Maria**, married Henry Zimmermann.
  - William.
  - Mary.
  - John.
  - Emma.
  - Sarah.
  - Louis.
  - Ida.
- **Adam**, married Mary Rolands.
  - Juliet, died.
  - Walter, died.
  - Addie Cornelia, died, married William Palmer.
- **Ellen**, married Simon Beard.
  - Mary.
  - Silas.
  - George.
  - Susan.
  - Harry.
- **Catharine**, died 1882, married John Jackson Cambell.
  - George.
  - Delia.
  - Nelson.
  - John.
- **Susan**, died, married George Price.
  - Alice.

CHILDREN OF MARX FORNEY AND HIS WIFE—CONTINUED.

JOHANN ADAM FORNEY AND ELISABETHA LOWISA ——.

MARX FORNEY AND BARBEL ——.

JOHANN ADAM FORNEY, born February 15, 1757, died June 21, 1834, married August 11, 1782, MARIA CHRISTINA HOFFMANN, born December 26, 1762, died June 15, 1810.

MARY CHRISTIANA, married ADAM FISHER.

Elizabeth, married John Zimmermann.
- Theophilus.
- Luther.
- Jeannette.
- Charles.
- Belle.
- John.

George, died, married, 1st, Emily Holtzman.
- Ida, married John Gettier.
- Edgar.

Married, 2d, Lizzie Emerich.
- George.

Married, 3d, Mary Bennett.
- Belle Bennett.
- Orville B.
- Nellie.
- Bessie.

Reuben, died.

Emaline, married Alexander Carns.
- Kate.
- Emaline.
- Nellie.
- Gertrude.
- Elsie.

ELIZABETH, born September 24, 1785, died Oct. 21, 1849, married MOSES LAMMOTT, born 1785, died May 29, 1848.

Levi Adam, born August, 1814, married September 19, 1843, Olive M. Armitage, died 1862.
- Mary Francis, died.
- Emma, died.
- Eugene Aurelius Ralph, born September 22, 1848, died September, 1883.
- Levi Forney, born 1850.
- Thomas A., born September 28, 1853.

Catharine, born 1818, died 1892, married Carl Erdmann.

JOHN ADAM, born October 8, 1789, died November 7, 1869, married LYDIA WIRT, born February 1, 1798, died February 22, 1852.

Abner Wirt, born February 8, 1819, married Louisa Wortz.
- David Franklin, married Annie Thomas.
  - Raymond.
  - William.
  - Claude.
  - Bertha.
  - Irene.
- Ezra Wirt, married Ada Snodgrass.
  - Wirt.
  - Elmo.
  - Robert.
- Lucie.

Catharine, born April 23, 1824, married David Sprenkle.
- Lydia Wirt, died June 10, 1879, married Emanuel Robert.
- Adam Forney.
- Enol, died 1886.
- Blaine, died 1881, married Laura Belle Eckert.
- Mary Elizabeth, married Edward Dubs.
- Herrington, died 1885.

Cornelius Wirt, born February 6, 1827, married Emily R. Cassell.
- Lillie, married George W. Riffell.
- Laura, married Jacob Dubs.
- Mary Ellen.
- Joseph H., married, 1st, Emma Rober, 2d, Louise Decker.

Lucretia Christiana, born August 22, 1829, married Lucian F. Melsheimer.
- John Adam, married Ella Trone.
  - Amelia.
  - Frederick.

Christian Wirt, born October 2, 1834, died February 2, 1853.

Lavina, born February 15, 1839, married Wm. Grove.
- Naomi.
- John.
- William.

LYDIA, married GEORGE STAIR.
- Adam F.
- Maria.
- George.
- Edward L.
- Walter.
- John.
- Sarah, died, married Lewis Smith.
  - Percy.
  - Menoth.
- Ezra.
- Henry.
- William, died 1891.

JULIANA, born 1794, died November 26, 1880.

ANNA MARGARET, born March 6, 1797, died March 7, 1881.

SUSANNA, born 1802, died February 12, 1891.

21

JOHN ADAM FORNEY married Maria Christina, daughter of Henry and Christina Hoffman. They lived on the farm now owned by Mr. Abner W. Forney and occupied by his son David. Subsequently they built the house afterwards known as the Pleasant Hill Hotel, but died in the small brick residence in which their three single daughters lived and died. The children of John Adam and Maria Christina (Hoffman) Forney were Catharine, Mary Christiana, Elizabeth, John Adam, Lydia, Juliana, Anna Margaret and Susanna.

CATHARINE FORNEY was married to David Newman, who was the son of a Prussian emigrant, and at one time kept a drug store in the room now occupied by J. L. Emlet for the same purpose; afterwards the Newmans moved to the vicinity of Cashtown, Adams county, where they kept a tavern on the top of "the Mountains" during the rest of their lives. They had ten children—Jesse David, Ephraim David, Ann Maria, Margaret, Michael, Adam Forney, James Ross, Lydia Ann, Julian and John David.

JESSE DAVID NEWMAN lived on the top of South Mountain, until after his second marriage, when he returned to Hanover and died there. By his first marriage with Catherine Kuhn he had five children—Thomas, Charles, Richard, Holliday and Matilda—who live in various parts of the country; by his second wife, Charlotte Stair, he had two children—Calvin and Lottie—who live in Hanover.

EPHRAIM DAVID NEWMAN resided on the South Mountain; he and his wife, Mary Sterner, have four children: Adam, George, Catherine and Amos, who reside in the vicinity, except Catherine (Newman) Byers, who lives in Chambersburg.

ANN MARIA NEWMAN is married to Peter Sholl, lives in Cashtown, and has one daughter, Kate.

MARGARET NEWMAN resides in Fayetteville, Pa., married to Abraham Brough, and has also one daughter, Harriet.

MICHAEL NEWMAN lives in Columbus, Ohio.

ADAM FORNEY NEWMAN lived in Wabash, Ind., where his widow and children still reside.

JAMES ROSS NEWMAN resided in Pittsburgh, where his sons, Franklin, James and John now live.

LYDIA ANN NEWMAN, married to Alexander Horner, resided in Finksburg, Md., where some of the family remain, others living in Baltimore and the West.

JULIAN NEWMAN, married to John Brown, lives in Fayetteville.

JOHN DAVID NEWMAN lives in Baltimore and has three children—Nettie, Ella and Jennie.

MARY CHRISTIANA FORNEY married Adam Fisher; they kept, at one time, a tavern in what is now called "the old hotel," on Pleasant Hill, in Hanover; subsequently they moved to Baltimore, where most of their children and descendants still live, with the exception of the eldest son and daughter. The eleven children of Adam and Mary Christiana (Forney) Fisher were Julian, Michael, Maria, Adam, Ellen, Catharine, Susan, Elizabeth, George, Reuben and Emaline.

JULIAN FISHER married Louis Michael, and, now a widow, lives in Hanover, where she has two married daughters.

22

MICHAEL FISHER also lives in Hanover, and has followed the occupation of a cabinet-maker all his life. To his recollections of old times and people, I am indebted for many details of the family history. He was married to Henrietta Stair, now deceased, and they have had eight children—Charlotte Elizabeth, Alice Josephine, Martha Marion, Michael, Eva, Emma, Kate and Gertrude.

MARIA FISHER, married to Henry Zimmermann, ELLEN, married to Simon Beard, and EMALINE, to Alexander Carns, are all living in Baltimore.

CATHARINE FISHER, married to J. J. Cambell, and SUSAN FISHER, married to George Price, also resided in Baltimore, but are now dead.

ELIZABETH FISHER is married to John Zimmermann, a brother of her sister Maria's husband, and resides in Harrisburg.

ADAM FISHER is now dead, as is his wife and their whole family.

REUBEN FISHER died unmarried.

GEORGE FISHER is also dead; he was thrice married, first, to Emily Holtzman, by whom he had a daughter, Ida, now married to John Gettier, and a son, Edgar; second, to Lizzie Emerich, by whom he had one son, George; and thirdly, to Mary Bennett, by whom he had four children, Belle, Orville, Nellie and Bessie.

ELIZABETH FORNEY was married to Moses Lammott, a grandson of Jean Henri La Motte, and son of his eldest son, Henry. Moses Lammott was usually called "Squire," and is still remembered as a courtly old man who used to come into Hanover from his farm in the full-costume of a gentleman of the period—ruffled shirt and all. He and his wife had two children—Levi Adam and Catharine.

LEVI ADAM LAMMOTT and his wife (nee Olive M. Armitage) had five children—Mary Francis, Emma, Eugene Aurelius Ralph, Levi Forney, and Thomas A. The daughters are dead; the two elder sons were in the Union army during the Civil War. EUGENE LAMMOT was the original of the character of the "Drummer Boy of Shiloh," although little of the play is taken from his life, except the fact of his youth and brave conduct in that engagement. His brother, Thos. A. Lamotte, of Philadelphia, writes: "He ran away from home (Marietta, O.), early in 1861, but returned because, he said, he could not go away without his mother's consent: she was then confined to her bed from which she never arose. She gave her consent, not, however, before, he standing at her bedside with her arms around him, she had his promise that he would do his duty. Years afterwards when asking my brother if he was not afraid in battle, he said he often felt like running, but his promise and mother's face seemed ever before him." He enlisted in the 77th Ohio, Colonel Hildebrand, which formed part of Sherman's Division at Shiloh. An old newspaper clipping tells the story: "It was Eugene Lammot who commenced beating the long roll at Pittsburg Landing. On that fatal day General Grant rode up and saw the little fellow standing out, with his drum strung on his boyish shoulders, and holding his drumsticks ready—'Can you beat the long roll, son?' mildly inquired Grant, while his eye rested on the little man. 'Yes, sir,' responded the boy, blushingly. 'Well, let them have it,' responded Grant, and in a moment the quick, rolling tara-tara, tat, tat, tara-tara was reverberating among the bluffs of the Tennessee. When the fight began, the boy took up a musket and fought like a tiger all day long. A rebel major galloped after him, demanding his surrender, but got for his reply a bullet through his heart, and Eugene Lammot became the hero of the day—the immortal Drummer Boy of Shiloh." Mr. Thomas Lamotte continues: "At the soldiers' reunion of 1874 I asked General Sherman if he remembered my brother. He said he remembered the circumstance of an Ohio drummer boy's bravery, but his regiment or name he could not tell. Eugene was afterwards captured, spending one day and night in the Tyler (Tex.) prison; escaping, he found his way back to his regiment, hiding by day, tramping, fording and swimming streams by night, possibly his youth was a help to him. * * * He was kind and generous to a fault; I never knew of his having an enemy and believe he was universally liked as a boy and dearly loved by his comrades in war. The seeds of consumption were no doubt implanted as a child in the army from exposure. I witnessed my brother's death (in St. Louis, in 1883); when asked where he wished to be buried, though scarcely conscious, he answered, 'With our mother.' His mother had been his guiding star." At his grave, Colonel Mason, of his old regiment said: "Quick to obey his superior officers, ever ready at the call of duty, he ceased to listen to his own drum taps that called the great army into battle at Shiloh, but joined the great silent majority now resting from strife across the river."

CATHARINE LAMMOTT was married to Carl Erdmann, of Hanover, where she recently died; the old Lammott farm is now in the possession of her husband. They had no children.

JOHN ADAM FORNEY married Lydia, daughter of Christian Wirt, previously mentioned; they lived on the farm now occupied by David F. Forney, probably a part of the original Forney tract; afterwards they moved into town and kept tavern on Pleasant Hill, as the successors of Adam Forney's sister, Mary (Forney) Fisher. There Lydia (Wirt) Forney died of consumption, and her husband subsequently lived with his daughter, Mrs. Melsheimer, where he ended his days. He was a soldier of the War of 1812, being one of the men who marched from Hanover to the defense of Baltimore in the company commanded by Captain John Bair.

The children of Adam and Lydia (Wirt) Forney were Abner Wirt, Catherine, Cornelius Wirt, Lucretia Christiana, Christian Wirt (who died in youth), and Lavina.

ABNER WIRT FORNEY resided on the farm owned by his father for many years; he then built his present residence in Hanover. He is married to Louisa Wortz; they have three children—David Franklin, Ezra Wirt and Lucie.

CATHARINE FORNEY was married to David Sprenkle, and lives, in widowhood, in Hanover. Of their six children, Lydia Wirt, Adam Forney, Ruel, Blaine, Mary Elizabeth and Hervington, but two, Forney and Mary, survive.

CORNELIUS WIRT FORNEY studied medicine, and for many years resided in Baltimore, but now lives in Hanover, where he was for nearly twenty years a justice of the peace. Dr. Forney and his wife (nee Emily R. Cassell), have four children—Lillie, Laura, Mary Ellen and Joseph H.

LUCRETIA CHRISTIANA FORNEY is married to Lucian F. Melsheimer, the son and grandson, respectively, of the Melsheimers, father and son, who are known as the "Fathers of American Entomology." His father, the Rev. John Frederick Melsheimer, was for twelve years the pastor of St. Matthew's, the oldest Lutheran church of Hanover, which his father, the Rev. Frederick Valentine Melsheimer, had served for twenty-five years before him. Both father and son were much interested in the science of whose study in America they were the pioneers; their valuable collections were bought for Harvard College, in 1864, by Prof. Agassiz.

Lucretia (Forney) Melsheimer and her husband have one son, John Adam, a practicing physician of Hanover, who inherits the scientific tastes of his forefathers. He and his wife (*nee* Ella Trone) have two children, Amelia and Frederick.

LAVINA FORNEY is married to William Grove, and lives in Baltimore; they have three children—Naomi, John and William.

LYDIA FORNEY, daughter of John Adam and Christina, married George Stahl, and resided, for a time at least, in Hanover. They had ten children who are now much scattered; Adam, Ezra and Henry residing in Cold Water, Mich.; Walter and John in Baltimore, where William lately died; Edward is a druggist in Chicago, while Sarah (now dead), was the wife of Lewis Smith, of Columbia City, Ind.

The younger daughters of John Adam and Christina Forney were JULIANA, ANNA MARGARET and SUSANNA. They remained single, and for many years led a very secluded life in their small brick dwelling in the midst of its garden. After the death of the last survivor of the sisters, many quaint and curious pieces of old furniture, clothing and china were brought to light, and the sale which followed Miss Susanna's death attracted buyers even from Baltimore.

Chapter III.

MARX FORNEY, AND DANIEL FORNEY, CHILDREN OF MARX FORNEY
AND GRAND CHILDREN OF JOHANN ADAM FORNEY.

JOHANN ADAM FORNEY AND ELISABETHA LOWISA ——.

MARX FORNEY, born April 6, 1760, died August 5, 1844, married ELIZABETH ZIEGLER, born 1771 (?), died March 10, 1852.

MARX FORNEY AND BARBEL ——.

GEORGE, born September 17, 1794.
MARGARET, born March 26, 1796, married Jos. HERSHEY.
ELIZABETH, born November 18, 1797, married JOHN BUTT.

MARKS, born November 14, 1799, died August, 1879, married ELIZA MARKS.
- Lovina, married Benjamin Kepner.
- Martha, married William Price.
- Lucy Ann, married J. Edward Schriver.
- J. Marks, married, 1st, —— Polley, 2d, —— Caldwell.

JACOB, born November 1, 1801.
MAGDALENA, born September 20, 1803, married JACOB MUSDORFF.
SALOME, born March 4, 1806, married JACOB PLANK.
SUSAN, married JACOB BREAM.
EVE, married SIMON MARKLE.
DANIEL, married LYDIA DEARDORFF.
EMANUEL, married —— RAHN.

MICHAEL, born 1789 (?), died November 18, 1861.

ANNA MARY, born August 10, 1793, died March 9, 1885, married —— SHRINER.
- Sally.
- Daniel, married —— Blizzard.
- Peter, married, 1st, Label McCullom; 2d, Kate Ness.
  - William.
  - John.
  - Edward.
- Margaret.
- Alfred.

SARAH, born August 28, 1795, died March 25, 1872, married DAVID WINCHESTER.
- Rebecca, born October 2, 1818, died April 21, 1841.
- Charles Barrel, born January 19, 1820, died 1845 (?).
- Sarah, born August 22, 1821, died March 15, 1872.
- William David, born September 5, 1823, died December 21, 1871, married Mary Currie.
  - Margaret Ella, married February, 1885, Marshall Sine.
    - Wm. Winchester.
    - Annie. } Twins.
    - Addie.
  - Sarah Frances, married 1887, Don Stewart.
    - Mary.
    - Ella.
- George Parks, born January 21, 1829, died April 25, 1841.
- George Lycurgus, born October 3, 1833, died April 21, 1863.

SUSANNA, } born 1800 { died 1863.
ELIZABETH, } { died March 5, 1884.

DANIEL FORNEY, born Aug. 17, 1762, died October 4, 1816, married SABINA SMYSER, born 1770, died September 29, 1847.

MARGARET, born January 18, 1802, died January, 1870, married December 16, 1822, RICHARD CROMWELL, born 1792, died November, 1864.
- Richard Hughes, born June 16, 1821, married Mary Jane Towner.
  - Nancy Margaret, married D. S. Batterton.
  - Sarah Agnes, married J. M. Brookbank.
  - William May.
  - Ella, married J. F. Armstrong.
  - Mary Rebekah, married Jos. Jaeger.
  - George Manderville, married Hattie Alexander.
  - Addie Davis, married Thomas Hargrave.
  - Virginia Bell, married George Reichel.
- Phebe Ellen, born December 18, 1826, died March 7, 1834.
- Daniel, born April 26, 1828, married Jane McPherson.
- Nathan Thomas, born February 8, 1830, married Sarah Strawn.
- Sally Ann, born October 15, 1831, died, married John Willis.
- Benjamin Franklin, born August 18, 1833, died.
- Margaret Ellen, born July 28, 1835, died July 29, 1868.
- Michael Forney, born August 22, 1837, married Emma Willis.
- Mary Elizabeth, born June 30, 1839.
- Susan Catharine, born October 8, 1841, married James Pierce.
- Jacob Forney, born October 19, 1843, married Lizzie Fenton.

JACOB S., born 1805, died November 1st, 1882.

DANIEL SMYSER, born 1808, married REBECCA CUMMINGS BUCHANAN.
- John, married Sarah Cracraft.
- Daniel Smyser, married, 1st, Henrietta Beatty; 2d, Syrene Gregory.
  - May, married —— Miller.
  - Irwin.
  - Frank Blair.
- Sarah, died, married Joseph W. Ferrell.
  - Wilbert, died.
  - Mary Rebecca, died.
  - Addie L., married —— McClure.
- Mary, married David L. Kelley.
  - Lee.
  - Willis.
  - Daniel.
- Nannie, married Frank Haughey.

JOHN, died in youth.

Of MARX FORNEY, son of Marx, little is known. He moved to Marsh Creek, west of Gettysburg, where his wife is buried, though he himself is interred in the old graveyard of the Reformed Church at Hanover. He and his wife, Elizabeth Ziegler, had eleven children: George, Margaret, Elizabeth, Marks, Jacob, Magdalena, Salome, Susan, Eve, Daniel and Emanuel. Two sons, George and Jacob, I suppose to have died in childhood: most of the other children lived in the vicinity of Gettysburg, with the exception of Emanuel, who resided and owned several farms, in Carroll Co., Md. Daniel is the only survivor of the family. Marks Forney, the younger, at the battle of Gettysburg, took into his house and nursed for six weeks, a wounded Confederate officer, who inquired the name of his host, and being told, said that *his* name was Forney: he thought himself a descendant of one of the Forney brothers who went south. This officer, Brigadier-General William H. Forney, has for many years represented the Seventh District of Alabama in Congress. I am inclined to think that he was mistaken in his genealogy. He is a descendant of the Huguenot family of Forneys who settled in North Carolina before the Revolution, and between them and the Forneys of Hanover there is no discoverable connection.

Marks Forney, the younger left a widow, now aged and blind, residing in Gettysburg with her daughter, Mrs. Schriver. There are four children: Lovina, married to Benjamin Kepner, and resident in Waynesboro': Martha (Mrs. Price); Lucy, the wife of J. Edward Schriver, of Gettysburg, who has given me most of the foregoing history, and J. Marx, who was first married to a Miss Polley and then to Miss Caldwell, and lives also at Gettysburg.

DANIEL FORNEY, son of Marx the elder, went to Frederick, Md., where he learned a trade, thence to York, where he married Sabina, daughter of Capt. Michael Smyser, a Revolutionary officer, serving in Col. Swope's regiment of militia, part of the "Flying Camp." Capt. Smyser was captured at Fort Washington on the disastrous taking of that fortress in 1776. He subsequently represented York County in the Pennsylvania legislature, was six times re-elected and afterwards served as State Senator. Daniel and Sabina (Smyser) Forney settled in Reisterstown, Md., in 1791, where for many years they kept a stage tavern of well-known excellence on the Baltimore pike.

They had nine children: Michael, Anna Mary, Sarah, Susanna and Elizabeth, Margaret, Jacob S., Daniel Smyser and John, (who died at school, in his nineteenth year.)

MICHAEL FORNEY resided at the old homestead in Reisterstown all his life and was never married. He served in the war of 1812.

ANNA MARY FORNEY married a Mr. Shriner, and her children were Sally, Daniel, Peter, Margaret and Alfred; but I have no further information concerning them.

SARAH FORNEY married a farmer, David Winchester, and they resided in Deer Park, Md. and York Haven after leaving Reisterstown. They had six children: Rebecca (who died young), Charles Burrell, who died unmarried, between twenty and thirty years of age, at Columbia, Mo.; Sarah, who also died unmarried; William David, who lived near Medon, Madison Co., Tenn., on a farm, was married to Mary Currie, and left two daughters: Mary Ella (Mrs. Sink), to whom I am indebted for this information, and Sarah Frances (Mrs. Stewart); George Parks died as a child and George Lycurgus Winchester went into the Confederate service as 2nd lieutenant, was afterwards made chaplain, and held this position at the time of his death; he died unmarried.

SUSANNA AND ELIZABETH FORNEY (who were twins) remained unmarried at the home in Reisterstown with their brothers Michael and Jacob.

MARGARET FORNEY married Richard Cromwell, son of Nathan and Phoebe (Bond) Cromwell. This family claim relationship with Thomas Cromwell, Henry VIII's Earl of Essex, and with Oliver Cromwell, the Protector. According to family tradition, "the King of England gave their ancestor a large grant of land near Baltimore to get that branch of Cromwells out of the country; Lord Baltimore's grant joined theirs on the east."

Richard and Margaret (Forney) Cromwell, who resided in Columbia, Mo., had eleven children: Richard Hughes, Phoebe Ellen, Daniel Forney, Nathan Thomas, Sarah Ann, Benjamin Franklin, Margaret Ellen, Michael Forney, Mary Elizabeth, Susan Catharine and Jacob Forney. Of these, Phoebe Ellen, Benjamin Franklin and Margaret Ellen died in childhood or youth.

RICHARD HUGHES CROMWELL, the eldest son, lives in Macon, Mo.; he is married to Mary Jane, daughter of Jacob Towner, of near Fairfax Courthouse, Va., and his wife, *nee* Pomroy. Richard Hughes and Mary (Towner) Cromwell have eight children: Nancy Margaret (who gave me this information), Sarah Agnes, William May, Ella, Mary Rebekah, George Manderville, Addie Davis and Virginia Bell.

DANIEL FORNEY CROMWELL is married to Jane McPherson, has four children, and lives in Moline, Ill., as does SUSAN CATHARINE CROMWELL, married to James Pearce, and JACOB FORNEY CROMWELL, married to Lizzie Fenton, now dead; neither of the latter have any children.

NATHAN THOMAS CROMWELL, married to Sarah Strawn, and living in Columbia, Mo., and MICHAEL FORNEY CROMWELL, married to Sarah Willis and living in the same place, are also childless. SARAH ANN CROMWELL married John Willis and has three children.

JACOB S. FORNEY was well educated as a civil engineer, but never practiced his profession. He was a very fine looking man, especially in his old age, being remarkably tall, as were all the family; he was six feet two; he and his unmarried sisters and brother lived in their large old house in the midst of their extensive lands, which stretch in all directions about the little town. In sight of the house, the liberality of the family erected a Lutheran church, of brick. They lived in considerable style, not keeping the tavern open; they held many slaves, to whom they willed money to build comfortable homes. The old house is now empty and deserted—a sad illustration of the inspired saying, "the fashion of this world passeth away."

DANIEL SMYSER FORNEY is the only survivor of the family. He is a graduate of Yale and practised medicine for many years in Burlington, Iowa, where, in advanced age, he still resides. He was married to Rebecca Cummings Buchanan, a relative of President Buchanan, and has five children: John, living on a farm near Bethany, W. Va.; Daniel Smyser, at Moberly, Mo.; Sarah, now deceased, married to Joseph Ferrell, of Wheeling, W. Va.; Mary, (Mrs. David L. Kelly) living in the suburbs of Chicago; and Nannie, (Mrs. Frank Haughey, of Reisterstown), to whose information I am indebted for most of the material of this chapter.

Chapter IV.

DESCENDANTS OF

NICOLAUS FORNEY, LOWISA CHARLOTTE (FORNEYS) SELL, MARIA EVA FORNEY, CLORA FORNEY, CHILDREN OF JOHANN ADAM FORNEY.

NICHOLAS FORNEY, the emigrant's second son, was born July 1, 1715, probably in Wachenheim; "his sponsor was the worthy Nickel Forney of Duerckheim," a larger town a few miles from Wachenheim. He was one of the four children with the parents in their emigration, being six years old when taken to Pennsylvania. He was brought up in the back woods "across Susquehanna," surrounded by the trials and hardships of pioneer life. He was married probably about 1742; his wife's name was Maria Magdalena; her family name is not known. In 1745 Nicholas Forney was arrested by Maryland officers sent by John Digges, for trespassing on the latter's land and cutting timber there; probably his father had given him a part of his own land, as the young man was now setting up a home of his own, and Nicholas cut down the trees to clear it. His father's account of the matter has already been given; apparently after the Maryland sheriffs were beaten off they made no further attempt to arrest Nicholas Forney but the consequences of the affair were more serious for his father. In 1752 we find Nicholas Forney's name in the list of those who held under Maryland rights in York county; "the Commissioners of York county undertook to collect taxes from the above as living north of the Temporary line but the Provincial authorities prevented it, on the ground that they held under Maryland rights and could not be taxed by Pennsylvania authority till the final settlement of the boundary line." In 1762 we find among the baptismal records of Jacob Lischy the following notice: "den 31sten May taufte abends Johan Niclaus Forny's Familie als Magdalena die Mutter Sophia Myerin Anna Margareth die Tochter Johan Adam Forny Barbara seine Frau Abraham Forny Philliph dito Heinrich dito Lowis dito Ester dito Joh. Niclaus dito Margareth dito." I cannot account for the remarkable fact that none of Nicholas Forney's family had been baptized in infancy; perhaps he had become tinctured with the opinions on infant baptism held by the "Dunkers" and Mennonites who were so numerous among the early German settlers of Pennsylvania, but afterwards changing his views, had his family baptized. He must have become interested in the Reformed Church, for we find his name among the subscribers to that undertaking, in 1764-5. In 1772 "Nicholas Forney of Manheim township"—now Heidelberg—was naturalised. At some time, Marx, his older brother, sold him a part of the land which their father had taken up on his Pennsylvania warrant. We do not know the date of Nicholas' death, but his wife is mentioned as a widow in 1774.

The children of Nicholas and Maria Magdalena Forney were Sophia, Johann Adam, Heinrich, Abraham, Margarethe, Philip, Lowis, Esther and Johann Nicolaus.

SOPHIA FORNEY was probably the eldest daughter, married to a Mr. Meyer, and I suppose Anna Margarethe to be their child; but I can find out nothing about her.

JOHANN ADAM FORNEY, probably the eldest son, and his wife Barbara, had five children. He and his brother Heinrich were subscribers to the building of the Reformed Church in 1764-5.

HEINRICH FORNEY and his wife Magdalena had at least two sons. In 1778 he was 2nd Lieutenant in the Seventh company of the Fourth Battallion of York County's militia.

ABRAHAM FORNEY and his wife Susanna had one daughter; but beyond this, which I get from the records of the Hanover Reformed church, I know nothing.

MARGARETHE FORNEY was married to Heinrich Bayer and they had a daughter, Maria Magdalena, to whom her grandmother, Nicholas Forney's wife, stood god-mother.

Of PHILIP and LOWIS FORNEY I know nothing; nor of ESTHER and JOHANN NICOLAUS, save that they were confirmed in the Reformed church in 1777, and that Esther, who stood god-mother to a child in 1778, was then single. Old people used to speak of a certain "Honnickle" Forney, who must have been Johann Nicolaus, and tradition has preserved the fact that he was a great narrator of ghost stories; but he himself has now faded into a ghost. I have not been able to discover any descendants of Nicholas and Magdalena Forney, which is remarkable, with so large a family. A tradition, preserved by Dr. D. S. Forney of the Reisterstown branch says that one of the Forney brothers went to Virginia.

LOWISA CHARLOTTE FORNEY, the emigrant's eldest daughter, was born in Wachenheim. "Her godmothers," writes the present town clerk, "were the two right honorable Fraülein von Blarer, of Geyersburg, one of the noble families in this place, whose former seat still stands, but has long since passed into other hands." Lowisa was married March 11, 1742, to Abraham Sell; I do not think that she lived long, or left any children; we find Sell's name in the Christ Church records, with another wife, in 1751.

MARIA EVA FORNEY, was, we know, at home when her father was arrested in 1747: and this is all we know about her.

CLORA FORNEY, I suppose to have died young: for a tradition speaks of the emigrant's family as consisting of three sons and *two* daughters.

Chapter V.

DESCENDENTS OF

PHILIP FORNEY, SON OF JOHANN ADAM FORNEY, AND ADAM FORNEY,
MARIA (FORNEY) SHRIVER, LOVICE (FORNEY) LEASE,
CHILDREN OF PHILIP FORNEY AND GRAND
CHILDREN OF JOHANN ADAM FORNEY.

CHILDREN OF PHILIP AND ELISABETH (SHERZ) FORNEY.

JOHANN ADAM FORNEY AND ELISABETHA LOWISA ——.

PHILIP FORNEY, born Sept. 29, 1724, died Feb. 3, 1783, married May 8th, 1753, ELISABETH SHERZ, born Feb. 6, 1732, died Aug. 8, 1791.

ADAM FORNEY, born June 15, 1754, died June 29, 1822, married October 28, 1784, RACHEL SHRIVER, born January 7, 1767, died December 7, 1845.

LYDIA, born January 11, 1786, died January 29, 1816, married August 1, 1802, JACOB WELCH.
- Rachel, born 1803, married Rev. James Baker.
- Charles, died 1846.
- Adam, born 1805.
- Christiana, born 1807, married George Little.
- Annie.
- Rebecca.
- Jacob.

DAVID SHRIVER, born November 4, 1787, died December 25, 1830, married 1st, January 23, 1812, ELIZABETH ZINN, died Mar. 25, 1816.
- John Zinn, born October 26, 1812, died March 4, 1859.
- Catharine, born October 1, 1815, married March 29, 1841, Daniel Zacharias.
  - Granville, died 1875.
  - John Forney.
  - Elizabeth Turbot, born June 14, 1840, married May 22, 1876, Thomas Justus Dunott, died May 20, 1893.
    - Justus, born June 5, 1867.
    - Daniel Zacharias, born February 11, 1870.
    - Catharine Forney, born June 13, 1872.
    - Sidney Paul Lancaster, born April 8, 1874.
  - Jane.
  - Lawrence Brengle.
  - Merle Herbine, died.
  - George Merle.
  - Edwin Daniel.
  - William.

Married, 2d, February 26, 1818, ELIZABETH DECKER, born May 26, 1789, died January 31, 1886.
- Mary, born December 28, 1819, married April 28, 1849, W. S. Roland.
  - Elizabeth, born October 10, 1842, married May 25, 1869, S. N. Jessof.
  - Anna M., born August 11, 1818, died August 29, 1849.
  - Catharine Forney, born October 22, 1852.
- Rebecca, born December 2, 1822, died December 27, 1843.
- Elisabeth, born October 18, 1824.
- Jacob D., born March 30, 1827, died December 14, 1872, married Elizabeth Adams.
  - Edward D., born December 8, 1852, married Rubie Stevenson.

SAMUEL, born March 6, 1790, married March 26, 1812, ELIZA SWOPE.
- Elizabeth, born December 12, 1812, married 1st, October 11, 1831, Jesse Gilbert, married 2d, May 8, 1845, Edward Buehler.
- Henry S., born February 1, 1815, married Maria Benson.
- Mary Jane, born February 12, 1817, married September 21, 1840, John C. Bridges.
- Louisa A., born October 24, 1819, married May 11, 1842, Horace Rathvon.
- Josephine, born November 7, 1825, married March 30, 1852, Wm. D. Roedel.
- David S., born January 9, 1828.
- John S., born February 17, 1830, married February 21, 1861, Mary Shriver.

ANNA MARIA, born June 23, 1792, died October 7, 1816.

REBECCA, born May 15, 1794, died April 26, 1881, married Eli Lewis, born September 30, 1789, died May 4, 1867.
- Mary Jane, born June 23, 1826.
- Alfred E., born September 16, 1842, married Mary Wolff.
  - Lucretia M., born March 18, 1865.
  - Alfred E., born February 20, 1867.
  - Mary Wolff, born February 19, 1869.
  - Ellis, born May 4, 1871.
  - Gerald, born December 6, 1873.
  - Frank, born April, 1876.
  - Edith, born February 20, 1879.
- Rebekah, born June 30, 1846, married Horace Bonham.
  - Mary Lewis, born April 14, 1871, died May 28, 1872.
  - Elizabeth Stayman, born November 2, 1872.
  - Amy Lewis, born June 16, 1874.
  - Eleanor Milton, born December 31, 1881.

JOHANN ADAM FORNEY AND ELISABETHA LOWISA——.

PHILIP AND ELISABETH (SHERZ) FORNEY.

ADAM FORNEY AND RACHEL SHRIVER.

Jacob, born February 1, 1797, died June 4, 1882, married June 25, 1829, ELIZABETH WINEBRENNER, born January 4, 1801, died November 17, 1861.

Ann Maria, born March 24, 1831, died February 18, 1834.
Adam, born June 7, 1833, died March 6, 1834.
Sarah, born January 31, 1835, died November 29, 1872.
David, born February 6, 1837, died March 12, 1843.
Mary, born June 8, 1839.
Emelia, born July 14, 1841, married June 29, 1870, William Shall Young.

William Forney, born April 17, 1871, died January 1, 1872.
Elizabeth Forney, born January 26, 1874.
Jacob Forney, born October 28, 1875.

Jacob, born March 3, 1844, died July 21, 1844.
Elizabeth Rebecca, born October 6, 1846, married March 5, 1882, George Young.

Joy Forney, born June 5, 1868.

Susanna, born April 11, 1799, died December 21, 1885, married DANIEL BARNITZ.

Alexander, born August 22, 1826.
Annie, born November 11, 1829, married Jacob Blymeyer.
William Tell, born September 29, 1830, died October, 1887.
Lewis.
Susan, born December, 1835.

Peter, born November 16, 1801, married Oct. 21, 1845, AMANDA [NACE] FORNEY.

Edward Otis, born May 1, 1847, married November 23, 1881, Anna Regina Hanna.

Joseph Raymund, born September 19, 1862.
Edward Francis, born December 12, 1884.

Lewis S., born May 26, 1805, died July 11, 1884, married November 1, 1832, MARY HOLLINGER, born November 5, 1811, died January 23, 1873.

Ann Maria, born October 12, 1833, married Henry J. Foltz.
Sarah, born February 17, 1835.
Joseph, born May 1, 1837, died May 15, 1837.
Jacob H., born September 3, 1838, married Annie E. Zeller.
Adam, born October 15, 1840, married June, 1871, Ada Dice.
William Henry, born September 20, 1843, died October 9, 1843.
Eliza Rebecca, born October 15, 1844.
Mary Clara, born October 16, 1846, married October 13, 1870, B. F. Wingard.
Amanda, born July 20, 1849, died March 8, 1881.
Lewis, born March 20, 1851, died April 21, 1851.
Eli Lewis, born December 21, 1852.

Sarah, born September 23, 1807, died January 8, 1878, married HENRY WINEBRENNER, born June 29, 1809, died March 25, 1886.

Peter Forney, born July 16, 1837, married February 28, 1889, Amelia E. Voyce.

David Edwin, born August 25, 1839, married Eliza Brengle Shriver.
Helen Shriver.
Martha Catharine.
David Edwin.

Mary, born August 9, 1841, married Henry Wirt Shriver.
Lucy (died in infancy.)
Elizabeth.
Henry Wirt.
Mary Winifred.
Sarah Catharine.

Sarah, born September 18, 1843.

Martha, born January 18, 1845.

H. Calvin, born July 6, 1848, married 1877, Emma Eckert.

MARIA FORNEY, born September 17, 1755, died September 14, 1804, married LUDWIG SHRIVER, born February 23, 1749, died September 16, 1804.

MARIA CATHARINA, born November 17, 1771, died November 5, 1849, married DANIEL GOBRECHT, born June 18, 1772, died March 5, 1842.

William D., born December 6, 1799, died May 31, 1859, married Amanda Miller, born November 11, 1802.

Neander Augustus, born September 7, 1851, married April 2, 1871, Clara Jane Beecher.

William Edward, born September 16, 1872, died January 11, 1873.
George Nevin, born December 9, 1874.
Carl Whitmer, born April 28, 1877, died July 27, 1879.
Samuel Beecher, born September 28, 1878.
Edwin Neander, born August 25, 1880.
Elmer Ellsworth, born March 30, 1881, died April 10, 1884.
Bertha May, born May 12, 1887, died August 21, 1887.
John Christopher, born September 14, 1888.
Clara Irene, born January 21, 1890.

LOVICE FORNEY, born April 26, 1757, died —— married LEONHARD LEASE.

GEORGE, married, 1st, MARIE STEINER. 2d, MARIA RINGGOLD.

Elizabeth, married —— Slack.
Harriet Rebecca, married William Medcalfe.
Jane, married —— Groves.
Maria, died 1886, married Hamilton G. Coward, died 1889.

PHILIP FORNEY, the youngest son of the emigrant, was the first of the family born in America, and might have been called, like that descendant of the Penns who was so entitled from being born here, the "American" Forney. He was born, probably, in Philadelphia County, but his early years were passed chiefly in "Conewago." He married Elisabeth Sherz (or Sharretts), who probably belonged to the family who for several generations owned "Sharretts' Mill," south of Hanover. Philip inherited the homestead farm, in accordance with the German custom of the "Minorat" prevalent in the Palatinate, which gives the homestead to the *youngest* son. He also owned land near Reistertown, Md., adjoining that of Marx Forney's son Daniel: this land he willed to furnish dowries of £50 each for his daughters who were single at the time of his death. Philip Forney and his wife are interred in the old Reformed graveyard at Hanover.

Philip and Elisabeth (Sherz) Forney had twelve children: Adam, Maria, Lovice, Elizabeth, Philip, Samuel, David, Peter, Hannah, Jacob, Susanna and Salome.

ADAM FORNEY married Rachel, daughter of David and Rebecca (Ferree) Shriver. She was a member of the family which was the next, after the Forneys, to settle in the neighborhood of what is now Hanover. Tradition tells how the Forneys, on their first settlement at 'Conewago," supposed themselves to be the only white people there, until one day they found in the woods a pig, and by the presence of a domestic animal knew that they had civilized neighbors, who afterwards proved to be the Shrivers. A descendant, Miss Mary Forney, of Hanover, from whose account given in the "History of the Shriver Family," the quotations in this chapter are taken, says "Adam Forney was engaged in the business of tanning. He was in comfortable circumstances, a man of strict integrity, genial manners and hospitable disposition. His wife was a woman of sterling worth, inclined to be what is now termed 'strong minded,' but in every respect a firm, conscientious and good woman." A tradition, preserved by Edward Otis Forney, of Washington, D. C., tells us that "Adam Forney, moved by patriotism, left his home in Hanover to join the American forces at Brandywine: but, being of a delicate constitution, he was, in a short time, brought home in a one-horse cart, being unable to endure the hardships of a soldier's life." He probably was not mustered into service, as his name does not appear upon any Revolutionary roll.

The children of Adam and Rachel (Shriver) Forney were: Lydia, David Shriver, Samuel, Anna Maria, Rebecca, Jacob, Susanna, Peter, Lewis S. and Sarah.

LYDIA FORNEY married Jacob Welsh, son of George Welsh, at one time Prothonotary of Adams County. They had seven children: Rachel, Charles, Adam, Christiana, Annie, Rebecca and Jacob.

DAVID SHRIVER FORNEY, says his daughter, Mrs. Roland, "when young, was in a leather store in Baltimore. While thus employed he formed the acquaintance of Mr. Zinn, of Harrisburg, and accepted the offer of a partnership in his tannery. He subsequently married Mr. Zinn's only daughter, Elizabeth. They had two children, John Zinn and Catharine." John Zinn Forney was a surgeon in the Mexican war: he was appointed by President Buchanan consul to Liberia, and died at Monrovia, six months after his arrival. He was unmarried. Catharine Forney was married to Daniel Zacharias, a prominent minister of the German Reformed church. He was a pastor at Frederick, Md., for forty years.

35

Their children are: Granville (who died in Colorado), John Forney and Edwin Daniel, living in Cumberland, Md.; Lawrence Breugle and William, both of New York; Elizabeth Turbot, married to Dr. Dunott, of Harrisburg; George Merle, a minister of the Reformed church; Jane, who lives in Baltimore and is much interested in various musical and charitable objects; and Merle Herbine, who died young. David Shriver Forney was married, a second time, to Elizabeth Decker, and moved to Carlisle. There he "had a tannery and farm, which he managed during his life. He was a good man—a great churchman." By his second marriage he had four children—Mary, Rebecca, Elisabeth and Jacob D., of whom the survivors are Mrs. Mary Roland and Miss Elisabeth Forney. Mrs. Dr. Roland has in her possession an old coin of the imperial city of Ratisbon, which has been passed from eldest son to eldest son in Philip Forney's branch of the family. Its present inheritor is Mr. Edward B. Forney, of Washington, D. C. It has a ring and ribbon to attach it around the neck, and the date—1691—is probably that of the emigrant Johann Adam's birth. It is said to have been used at his marriage, in accordance with the old Teutonic custom, a relic of marriage by purchase, in which the groom gave a piece of money instead of a ring to his bride.

SAMUEL FORNEY was a druggist in Gettysburg; he was commonly called "Doctor," though not a physician. He was married to Eliza Swope, and their children were Elizabeth, Henry S., Mary Jane, Louisa A., Josephine, David S. and John S.

ANNA MARIA FORNEY, called Polly, "was reported beautiful in person, amiable and lovely in disposition and manners. Her death was especially sad, being very sudden, her funeral occurring on the day of her appointed marriage."

"REBECCA FORNEY, the wife of Eli Lewis, was a woman of fine sensibilities, beautifully dignified in manners, and kind and genial in disposition." Mr. Lewis was, for a time, the editor of the "Baltimore Patriot." He was also postmaster of Baltimore. They had three children: Mary Jane, Alfred E. and Rebekah.

MARY JANE LEWIS resides in Philadelphia.

ALFRED E. LEWIS graduated from Princeton in 1853, was admitted to the York bar and practiced his profession until the outbreak of the war, when he raised a company of volunteers in York, which became Battery E., First Penna. Artillery. He served on General McAll's staff, and was mentioned in orders for his "gallant and distinguished services" after the battle of Gaines' Mill. Major Lewis left the army in 1863, and has lived in Philadelphia most of his life, with the exception of three years, when he was Deputy Fifth Auditor of the Treasury, being appointed by President Cleveland. Since his retirement from office he has lived in Milford, Pa. He is married to Mary Wolff, and they have seven children.

REBEKAH LEWIS married Horace Bonham, an artist, of York, where, in widowhood, she resides with her three daughters.

JACOB FORNEY "commenced life as a tanner, but after some years turned his attention to farming. He was a man of great energy and fine business qualifications, and was mainly instrumental in building the Hanover Branch Railroad, and in establishing the First National Bank of Hanover, with which corporation he was connected up to the time of his death. Elizabeth Winebrenner, his wife, was a woman of many virtues, a sweetly amiable and good character." They had seven children, of whom Ann Maria, Adam, David and Jacob died in childhood, Sara in middle life and unmarried; Emelia is married to William S. Young, of Baltimore, and Elizabeth to George Young, his son by a previous marriage. I have already referred to the interest in family history taken by Miss Mary Forney, who still resides in the homestead at Hanover.

SUSANNA FORNEY was the second wife of Daniel Barnitz, of Hanover; of their five children, Alexander lived in Baltimore; Ann, married to Jacob Blymeyer, at Lewistown William and Lewis at Tullahoma, Tenn., and Susan in Hanover. All but the two last named are now dead.

PETER FORNEY, like most of the family, was a tanner in early life, but afterwards went into the wholesale grocery business of his uncle, Peter Forney, in Baltimore. Returning to Hanover, he married Amanda (Nace) Forney, the widow of Matthias Nace Forney, hereafter mentioned. They had one child, Edward Otis; he is a graduate of Franklin and Marshall College, entered the German Reformed ministry, and was pastor of of churches at Shepherdstown, Va. and Norristown; became a Catholic and now resides in Washington, being an assistant examiner in the Patent Office. He is married to Anna Regina Hanna, and they have two sons—Raymund and Edward.

LEWIS S. FORNEY carried on the family occupation of tanning at Waynesboro'. He was married to Mary Hollinger and, of their eleven children, Adam, Ann Maria (Mrs. Foltz), Sarah, Eliza and Amanda still reside there; Jacob lives in Baltimore. Mary Clara (Mrs. Wingard) in Chicago, and Eli in York.

Of SARAH FORNEY her niece says: "She lived out the allotted three score and ten years wherein life can be bright and happy, and surely few lives have shown greater friendliness, cheeriness and contentment." She married Henry Winebrenner, a brother of Jacob Forney's wife. They had six children, of whom Peter Forney and Calvin are in business in Baltimore, David in Hanover, Mary is married to H. Wirt Shriver, of Union Mills, Md., who has been previously mentioned; the Misses Sarah and Martha Winebrenner occupy the family home, in which during the war they had the thrilling experience told in a contemporary letter of F. Austin Shriver's: "During the skirmish in Hanover between Stuart's and Kilpatrick's cavalry, there was a rebel battery about 800 yards from Henry Winebrenner's house which shot a shell through their up-stairs back porch door, descending to the kitchen where the whole family were collected; but the shell did not explode and, almost miraculously, none of the family were injured."

MARIA FORNEY, daughter of Philip, was married to Ludwig Shriver, a son of Ludwig and Anna Maria Schreiber, and a cousin of Rachel (Shriver) Forney's father. The younger Ludwig's name is found among the subscribers to the building of the Reformed church in Hanover in 1764–5; he also donated rafters for the school-house, for which contributions were received in kind. As appears from the tax-list of 1783, he owned a grist-mill, probably the one now known as "Basehoar's Mill," near Christ Church. He and his wife died within two days of each other, and they have a double grave-stone in the old grave yard of Hanover, whose inscription tells us that "they were lovely in their lives and in their death were not parted."

Ludwig and Maria (Forney) Shriver were survived by several children but I have the record of only one, CATHARINE, who married Daniel Gobrecht, the eldest son of the Reverend John Christopher Gobrecht, for years the minister of the Reformed church in Hanover. He is said to have been an ardent patriot, preaching to the Revolutionary soldiers before they left for the war, on their duties as men and citizens; an account of him may be found in Harbaugh's "Lives of the Fathers of the Reformed Church." His son Daniel was a druggist, having a shop on Baltimore Street, where he also conducted the affairs of the Hanover circulating library, whose books were exchanged at his store. His wife Catharine is described as a small, prepossessing-looking woman.

Daniel and Catharine (Shriver) Gobrecht had but one child, WILLIAM D., (the middle initial being assumed to distinguish him from his father's brother.) William D. Gobrecht was a lawyer, a man of intelligence and fine manners; he spent most of his life in Hanover, then removed to Arendtsville, Adams County, where he married Amanda, daughter of John F. and Louisa Miller, and where he died, leaving one son, Neander Augustus. His widow has since remarried.

NEANDER AUGUSTUS GOBRECHT began a collegiate course with a view to the ministry, but, owing to a throat trouble, relinquished it and learned carpentry. He has furnished me with very full and accurate accounts of his family. He is now a resident of Altoona, is married to Clara J. Beecher, and has had nine children, four of whom are dead.

LOVICE FORNEY married Leonhard Lease. They had, I am told, only one son, GEORGE LEASE, who was a merchant in Carlisle; he married, first, Marie Steiner, of Frederick, Md., and they had one child, Elizabeth; after her mother's death, her grandmother took Elizabeth Lease to Frederick, where she lived until married to Mr. Slack, of Cumberland. She is now dead and I have no information of any descendants. George Lease's second wife was Maria Ringgold, of the Eastern Shore of Maryland. "Traditions of their gay marriage told how a party of their friends accompanied them from Baltimore to Carlisle, and how, when they reached their future home all the bells in the place were rung and guns fired; there were great demonstrations to announce the arrival of the wedding party."

George and Maria (Ringgold) Lease had three daughters: Harriet Rebecca, (who married William Medcalfe, M. D.); Jane, (who married the Rev. Mr. Groves); and Maria, who married Hamilton Coward and moved to California where both of them died, leaving four sons. After George Lease's death his widow married a Mr. Stump, a man much older than herself, who died shortly after their marriage; they had no children.

Chapter VI.

———

DESCENDENTS OF

ELIZABETH (FORNEY) LAMMOT, DAUGHTER OF PHILIP FORNEY, AND
GRAND DAUGHTER OF JOHANN ADAM FORNEY.

CHILDREN OF PHILIP AND ELISABETH (SHERZ) FORNEY—CONTINUED.

JOHANN ADAM FORNEY AND ELISABETHA LOWISA —

PHILIP AND ELISABETH (SHERZ) FORNEY.

ELIZABETH, born July 12, 1779, died May 9, 1862, married 1st, GEORGE SOWERS, married, 2d, —— ELLIOTT.

Daughter, married —— Spaulding.

Several daughters.

ELIZABETH, born October 4, 1758, died September 24, 1865, married October 1778. DANIEL LAMMOT, born May 10, 1748, died May 2, 1812.

DANIEL, born September 11, 1782, died September 20, 1877, married May 15, 1805, SUSANNA BECK, born November 10, 1786, died December 31, 1847.

Margaretta Elizabeth, born April 29, 1807, married October 28, 1824, Alfred Victor Du Pont, born April 11, 1798, died October 4, 1856.

William, born May 8, 1850, died August 16, 1874.

Meta, born May 3, 1852, married { Judith.
Lockwood de Forrest.   Alfred Victor.

Mary Charlotte, born September 25, 1854, married Henry A. Smonds.
Peter, born June 22, 1857.
Richard Law, born November 24, 1865.

Victorine Elizabeth, born August 18, 1825, died, married January 18, 1849, Peter Kemble, died.

Paulina Emma, born July 23, 1827.

Eleuthère Irénée, born August 3, 1829, died September 17, 1877, married October 28, 1850, Charlotte Shepherd Henderson, born September 24, 1823, died August 19, 1877.

Anna Cazenove, born May 1, 1860, married Absalom Waller.

Marguerite, born December 21, 1862, married September 20, 1881, Cazenove G. Lee. { Cazenove.
Maurice Du Pont.

Alfred, born May 12, 1864, married Bessie Gardner.
Maurice, born May 8, 1866, married Margery Fitzgerald.
Louis Cazenove, born January 27, 1868, died 1892.

Lammot, born April 13, 1831, died March 29, 1884, married October 3, 1865, Mary Belin, born September 29, 1839.

Isabella, born October 22, 1866, died June 29, 1871.
Louisa d'Andelot, born June 25, 1868.
Pierre Samuel, born January 15, 1870.
Sophia Madeleine, born May 29, 1871.
Henry Belin, born November 5, 1873.
William Kemble, born March 29, 1875.
Pierre, born December 21, 1876.
Mary Alletta, born November 20, 1878.
Lammot, born October 12, 1880.
Isabella, born May 31, 1882.
Margaretta Lammot, born May 12, 1884.

Alfred Victor, born April 18, 1822, died 1893.

Sophie Marie, born December 3, 1834, died December 27, 1869, married Charles Irénée Du Pont, born August 5, 1830, died January 7, 1873.

Victorine Antoinette, born January 29, 1863, died November, 1876.
Philip Charles, died.

Biderman, born October 13, 1837, married Ellen S. Coleman, died May 10, 1876.

Margaretta Elizabeth, married B. Coleman.
Coleman, married Alice Du Pont.
Bidermann, married Ethel Clark.
Bora.
Zara.
Paulina.
Evan.

CHILDREN OF PHILIP AND ELISABETH (SHERZ) FORNEY—CONTINUED.

JOHANN ADAM FORNEY AND ELISABETHA LOWISA —

PHILIP AND ELISABETH [SHERZ] FORNEY.

Allen, born September 20, 1812, died February 27, 1815.

Ferdinand Fairfax, born September 7, 1808, died January 24, 1810, married December, 1844, Marietta Allen, born December 21, 1812, died July, 1850.

Isabella, born January 20, 1871, died June 21, 1871.
Alice, born July 13, 1872.
Henry, born November 19, 1873, died July 11, 1878.
Paul, born July 28, 1875.
Charles, born June 26, 1877.
Ferdinand La Motte, born March 15, 1881.

Margaretta Elizabeth, born December 28, 1846, married September 13 1868, Henry Bella, born September 3, 1843.

Ellen, born November 27, 1852.
Augusta, born June 19, 1870.
Ferdinand, born December 10, 1880.
Victor, born June 20, 1872, married February 4, 1849, Josephine Anderson.
Victor, born February 19, 1882.

Ferdinand, born October 31, 1844, married June 17, 1872, Ellen Newbold.

Mary Augusta, born November 20, 1811, married October 25, 182, Thomas Hounsfield.

Alice, born December 7, 1853.
William.
Ethel, born June 15, 1857, married H. M. Barksdale.
Charles L. born August 15, 1859.
Samuel Francis, born November 20, 1861, died September 19, 1862.
Alice, born October 15, 1863, married Coleman du Pont.
Francis, born June 14 1865.
Greta, born August 25, 1866, died December 21, 1873.
Sophie, born April 8, 1871.
René de Pelport, born February 25, 1874.

Alice, born December 7, 1853, married October 16, 1851, Victor Du Pont, born May 11, 1828, died.

Edgar, born October 7, 1856, married January 1, 1878, John H. Kent, born January 24, 1842.

Mary Augusta, born November 17, 1855, Kent, born March 16, 1872.
Lammot Du Pont, born November 15, 1879.

Margaretta du Pont, born September 12, 1845, died February 4, February, 1866 married Alexis I. Du Pont.

ELIZABETH FORNEY AND DANIEL LAMMOT.

DANIEL LAMMOT AND SUSANNA BECK.

Pauline Elizabeth, born December 5, 1842, died September 13, 1857, married April 22, 1857, George Churchman.

Edward G., born April 14, 1858.
Eleanora, born September 7, 1859.
Albert, born September 17, 1859.
Charles E., born December 27, 1861.

Elmora Adelaide, born May 7, 1814, died November 10, 1874, married October, 1841, Edward Woodward Gilpin, born July 15, 1818, died April 29, 1876.

Daniel, died June 2, 1853, married May 6, 1834, Indiana De Merainville.

Robert, born March 6, 1854, married November 29, 1882, Edward Hazlehurst.
Daniel, born April 10, 1856, married to the Hazlehurst.
Charles N., born July 4, 1857.
Eugene, born June 29, 1861.
Theodore Bevin, born March 24, 1862.
Julia, born April 30, 1866.

Eugenia Victorine, born August 21, 1822, died September 8, 1857.

Robert Smith, born August 21, 1825, married December 19, 1845, Ellen Cox, born March 21, 1827, died March 19, 1881.

Harry, born October 19, 1866.
Arthur, born June 24, 1871.
Clarence King, born May 21, 1876.

William Alexander, born December 1, 1828, married October 1, 1852, Anna Rebecca, born October 26, 1829.

Married, 24, December 7, 1810, ANNA POTTS SMITH, died July 25, 1851.

Harry Biller, born September 6, 1830, married May 1, 1852, Catharine Clayton, born October 2, 1841.

Robert Smith, born April 26, 1853.
Henry Clayton, born May 8, 1866.
Eugenia V., born March 1, 1868.
Emily Septim, born May 21, 1870.
William, born October 22, 1872, died January 12, 1877.
Anna E., born May 17, 1881.

Francis Forney, born June 25, 1832, died October 17, 1833.

Alfred Victor, born August 28, 1836, married May 18, 1870, Susan Formentle.

Edith, born May 21, 1871.
Victor, born May 27, 1872.
Gertrude, born November 10, 1875.
Constance, born April 5, 1879.
Alfred, born December 30, 1880.

Charles Eugene, born August 20, 1839, died —

40

ELIZABETH FORNEY, who is said to have been a very elegant, lady-like woman, was married to Daniel LaMotte, the second son of Jean Henri LaMotte, a French Protestant who, after he came to America, became a Mennonite. He never would tell his children anything of his family, saying that they were proud enough without knowing anything about it, but adding: "If you do not disgrace your family, it will never disgrace you." An uncle of his, Nicolas de LaMotte, came over during the Revolution with Rochambeau, and sent word to Jean Henri to come and see him, but the Mennonite refused on the ground that he was a man of peace, while Nicolas was a man of war. Nicolas, who was childless, wished to adopt one of Jean Henri's four sons, but this the father also refused. His grand-daughter, Mrs. du Pont, recollects Daniel LaMotte as a stout man, with knee-buckles and small clothes, who lived at the corner of Pearl and Fayette Streets in Baltimore, near the homes of David Forney and of Salome (Forney) Grove.

Daniel and Elizabeth (Forney) LaMotte had two children, Elizabeth and Daniel.

ELIZABETH LaMotte married first, George Sowers of Baltimore, a descendant of Christoph Saur, the pioneer printer of Pennsylvania, the first to publish a Bible in any European tongue on this continent; he printed in 1743 the fine quarto "Germantown Bible" in German; his literary and political activities and those of his son are described at length by Prof. Oswald Seidensticker, in his excellent sketches of Pennsylvanian history, "Bilder aus der deutsch-pennsylvanischen Geschichte."

George and Elizabeth (LaMotte) Sowers had one daughter, who married Mr. Spaulding, a Catholic gentleman of Baltimore; they had several daughters, all of whom died unmarried, some of them having entered a religious sisterhood, and the family is now extinct. After her first husband's death, Mrs. Sowers married a Mr. Elliott; they had no children.

DANIEL LAMMOT—so he spelt his name—was first married to Susanna, daughter of Paul Beck, a merchant of Philadelphia. He was well educated and a fine violinist. He spoke French and German so well that he was often called upon in Philadelphia, where he lived for some time, to act as interpreter to foreign visitors. He had studied French with the intention of going to France to claim an inheritance there, but his mother was so apprehensive of the dangers of the voyage that the plan was given up. Daniel and Susanna (Beck) Lammot had four children: Margaretta Elizabeth, Ferdinand Fairfax, Mary Augusta and Elenora Adelaide. By his second marriage with Anna Potts Smith, Daniel Lammot had nine children—Daniel, Eugenia Victorine (who died in youth), Robert Smith, William Alexander, Anna Rebecca, Harry Didier, Francis Forney (who died in infancy), Alfred Victor and Charles Eugene. "A very remarkable circumstance," writes his daughter, Mrs. du Pont, "was his celebrating his golden wedding with his second wife, an event I never heard of before; he lived to be ninety-five years old."

MARGARETTA ELIZABETH LAMMOT, to whose vivid and accurate recollections I am indebted for much of the material of this chapter, was married to Alfred Victor du Pont, son of Eleuthère Irénée du Pont de Nemours. This gentleman owed his remarkable Christian names to the suggestion of the philosopher Turgot, a friend of his father: but when the Revolution failed to bring the expected freedom and peace, the family emigrated to this country, arriving here on New Year's day, 1800, in a starving condition, for their

41

vessel had been long overdue and their provisions were exhausted. M. du Pont put off from the ship as soon as it approached the harbor of Newport, R. I., rushed to the nearest house, where the family were at breakfast, and, unable to explain himself in English, he snatched from the table the cornbread which formed the meal and took it to his suffering family. The surprise of the New England people, thus interrupted in their meal, may be imagined. Some time after landing, M. du Pont's attention was accidentally called to the poor quality of the powder made in this country. He was a pupil and assistant of Lavoiser, and had superintended the powder mills of the French government, so he resolved to start a powder mill, and after traveling over the country in search of a site, he selected the water-power of the Brandywine near Wilmington, Del. The inhabitants laughed at, or pitied the "crazy Frenchman" who purchased the rocky tract, built himself a stone house which he named "Nemours," and founded there the business in which his family, to the third generation, are still engaged. The powder mills are the largest in the world. At "Nemours" he entertained distinguished French visitors, such as Marshal Grouchy and LaFayette. Mrs. Alfred du Pont remembers how the young officers of the suite, arriving after dark, threw themselves upon the grass, exclaiming how cool and refreshing it was, when in fact the grass was brown by a protracted drought. M. du Pont de Nemours was a man of great benevolence and worth, characteristics inherited by his son, Alfred Victor du Pont, born in Paris, but brought to America in infancy.

The children of Alfred Victor and Margaretta Elizabeth (Lammot) du Pont are Victorine Elizabeth, Paulina Emma, Eleuthère Irénée, Lammot, Alfred Victor, Sophie Marie and Biderman.

Victorine Elizabeth du Pont married Peter Kemble, a connection of the famous Kemble family of England; both are now dead, leaving five children: William (now dead), Meta, Mary Charlotte, Peter and Richard Law.

Paulina Emma du Pont resides with her mother at their house, "Goodstay," near Wilmington.

Eleuthère Irénée du Pont married Charlotte Henderson; they are both dead, and their five children, Anna, Marguerite, Alfred, Maurice and Louis Cazenove (now dead), were brought up by their grandmother, Mrs. du Pont.

Lammot du Pont was engaged in the superintendency of the powder works: he conducted, for the government all the experiments for testing the efficiency and strength of new brands of powder. During the Civil War, he raised a company of "three months men," but was only in the army for a short time, soon returning to the works where he and his family could render more valuable service to the government. He was killed by an explosion of dynamite in 1884. His widow (nee Mary Belin) and ten children survive him.

Alfred Victor du Pont resided in Louisville, Ky., where he gifted the city with fine industrial schools. He was unmarried.

Sophia Marie du Pont married Charles Irénée du Pont, her cousin; they had two children, who, as well as their parents, are now dead.

Biderman du Pont, who resides in Louisville, was married to Ellen Coleman, now dead, and has seven children—Margaretta Elizabeth, Coleman, Biderman, Dora, Zara, Paulina and Evan.

FERDINAND FAIRFAX LAMMOT, the only son of Daniel and Susanna (Beck) Lammot, married Marietta Allen, of Maine, and had three children: Allen, who died in childhood, Margaretta Elizabeth, married to Henry Bolin, and Ferdinand, married to Ellen Newbold.

MARY AUGUSTA LAMMOT married Thomas Hounsfield, an Englishman; they have two children: Alice and Edgar. Alice married Victor du Pont: he studied law under Chief Justice Gilpin, his uncle, and practiced in Wilmington, where he died much esteemed, leaving a widow and eight children. Edgar is married to Jane D. Kent; they have a daughter and two sons.

ELENORA ADELAIDE LAMMOT married Edward W. Gilpin, a prominent lawyer, who became Attorney-General, and afterwards was for twenty years, Chief-Justice, of Delaware. He and his wife, who were most devoted to one another, died within a short space of time, leaving two daughters, Margaretta du Pont, married to Alexis I. du Pont, and Paulina Elizabeth, who married George Churchman, and is now dead, leaving four children.

DANIEL LA MOTTE, the oldest child of Daniel Lammot's second marriage with Anna P. Smith, was married to Dolores de Murguiando, and had six children: Dolores (Lolita), Daniel, Charles, Eugene, Theodore and Julia.

ROBERT SMITH LA MOTTE served in the army during the Civil War, and was subsequently an officer in the regular army; Fort Ellis, Montana, was built under his supervision. He was married to Ellen Cist, and has three sons—Harry, Arthur and Clarence.

WILLIAM LA MOTTE was also in the army during the war; he and his sister ANNA reside, unmarried, in Wilmington.

HARRY DIDIER LA MOTTE lives in California: he is married to Catherine Clayton, and has had six children—Robert, Harry, William (deceased), Eugenia, Emily and Anna.

ALFRED LA MOTTE also lives in California: he and his wife, Susan Formahls, have five children: Edith, Victor, Gertrude, Constance and Alfred.

CHARLES EUGENE LA MOTTE was, during the war, the colonel of the 1st U. S. V. V., and was brevetted a brigadier-general of volunteers: he was greatly interested in family history, and during the latter years of his life, when an invalid, he occupied himself in the collection of much of interest and value respecting his own family and those related to it. I have had access to much of this material, which has been of great service. General La Motte died unmarried.

Chapter VII.

———

DESCENDANTS OF

PHILIP FORNEY AND SAMUEL FORNEY, SONS OF PHILIP FORNEY, AND
GRAND SONS OF JOHANN ADAM FORNEY.

JOHANN ADAM FORNEY AND ELISABETHA LOWISA ——.

PHILIP FORNEY, born July 7, 1760, died young.

PHILIP AND ELISABETH (SHERZ) FORNEY.

SAMUEL FORNEY, born April 21, 1762, died August 27, 1844, married SUSANNA KARLE, born April 14, 1767, died August 29, 1843.

GEORGE, born July 21, 1789, died March 27, 1849, married ELIZABETH YOUNG, born July 2, 1795, died April 27, 1850.

Josiah, died December 24, 1881, married Sarah ——.
Henry Clay.

Angelina, married Abraham Rife.
Ephraim Forney, married Jennie Felty.
Claude Merwin. Edna. Bessie.
Helen Elizabeth, married Winfield Scott Schroeder.
Carrie Marie.

Ephraim, married ——.
Clyde.

Jesse, married Catharine Feaser.
David. Lillie Frances (died in infancy). Karle Herbert (died in infancy). Luella (died in infancy). Georgie. Lutie.

James Henry, died May 23, 1892, married Margaret Allewelt.
Leander. Adolphus. Bella. Cora.

Adolphus, married Mary Diehl.
Harrison. Alfred. Leander.

JOHN, born March 25, 1792, died young.

ELIZABETH, born November 5, 1793, died 1868, married DAVID SHULTZ.

Cornelia, died 1889.
Walter Forney, married Annie ——.
Elizabeth Forney, married William King.
Maria.
David Augustus, died young.

JESSE, born 1801, died August 15, 1818.

HELENA, born May 18, 1803, died August 27, 1804.

KARLE, born October 19, 1810, died March 28, 1887, married MARY ANN HAY, died June 29, 1893.

Samuel Hay, married Mary Young.
Mary Margaret. Laura Grace. Lizzie Blanche.

William Granville, married Mary Dillard.

Susan, died June 18, 1874, married Andrew Bellune.
Fanny. Helen (died in infancy).

John Wogan, married Lizzie Beatty.

Robert Lee, married Mary King.

George Franklin.

PHILIP FORNEY, son of Philip, probably died young, as there is no mention of him among the four sons enumerated in his father's will.

SAMUEL FORNEY lived on the old Forney farm near the site of the "long log-house" which Mr. Michael Fisher remembers as standing under the willow trees at the chain of springs in the "little meadow," on the site of the present spring-house; the original stable stood on the rising ground to the west, where the present house stands. There was an old pear tree, traditionally said to have been brought from Germany, which stood, within the memory of living persons, at the back porch of the log-house. In the spring at the edge of the grove in the large meadow, the Indian mothers were said by Mrs. Samuel Forney to have bathed their papooses. A few rods west of the old house Samuel Forney built (about 1810) a sightly colonial mansion for himself. He was the last person in York county who owned a slave; this latest survivor of slavery in this section—"old Uncle Sam"—died in 1841; the small houses on the Westminster road, just before it entered the Frederick road, were originally built as slave quarters. Samuel

Forney lost his sight from an injury caused by a nail striking him in the eye, on March 21, 1832; he lived after this misfortune about twelve years. His wife was Susanna, daughter of George Adam Karle.

The children of Samuel and Susanna (Karle) Forney were George, John (who died young), Elizabeth, Jesse (who also died in youth), Helena (who died in infancy), and Karle.

GEORGE FORNEY lived on a farm now owned by a Mr. Hershey, along the line of the "Short Line" railroad, near Hanover. He was married to Elizabeth, daughter of Henry Young, and had six children—Josiah, Angelina, Ephraim, Jesse, James Henry and Adolphus. The family, after their parents' death, moved to Peoria county, Ill., where most of them still reside. The only daughter, Angelina, was married to Abraham Rife, and lives a few miles from Hanover. Josiah died while on a visit to his old home, and is buried beside his parents in the Lutheran churchyard in Hanover: James Henry is also dead. Adolphus lives in Kansas.

ELIZABETH FORNEY was married to David Shultz, a gifted lawyer of Hanover. She was a woman of great spirit, firmness and strong family pride. During the latter part of her life she lived in Gettysburg, on Seminary Ridge, the scene of the first day's fight. Her daughter, Miss Maria, gives this account of their experience during the battle: "We expected only a skirmish between raiders when the opening crash began, but were carried along with the excitement and laughed to see the crowds of civilians and non-combatants fly before the retreating and hard-pressed soldiery, until all the fences went down and the cavalry drew up around the house, in the yard, and the bullets crashed into the front and back windows, and the dead, dying and wounded lay all around. A few minutes later, Generals Lane and Thomas stood at the door, speaking to me, when General Pender and Captain Adams, of his staff, rode up, and General Thomas explained to them that there were three ladies entirely alone, and as I had asked for the hospital flag which Captain Adams had under his arm—having mistaken it for a battle flag—he kindly gave it to me, when I told him it was only an old red shawl of mother's. While I was entertaining the Southern officers at the back door, mother (who was seventy-odd years old) and Cornelia were in the front of the house with the surgeons and Union wounded who were being carried away as fast as possible, and had not yet learned that the southern army held possession. Amid the confusion and excitement, the day passed rapidly and closed, finding us in the middle of the victorious army, with every man ready to help or provide for us if need be and attend to the few wounded left behind in the hurried flight. After night I was called on to take the lamp and go down into the cellar with Adjutant Whitaker of North Carolina, to hunt for concealed prisoners, but found none. We passed through the next three days in the midst of the army, receiving the most considerate attention from all, general officers and men. All of us were highly complimented on our courage."

The children of David and Elizabeth (Forney) Shultz were five in number— Cornelia, now dead; Walter Forney, also deceased, who resided in Philadelphia; Elizabeth Forney, married to Mr. King and living in Texas; Maria, residing in Gettysburg, and David Augustus, who served in the Union army, rising to the rank of Major of the 73d Pa., and died shortly after the close of the war.

46

KARLE FORNEY, who was named for his mother's family, lived in Hanover, on the original Forney tract which is now owned by his son, Samuel Hay Forney; it has been in the uninterrupted possession of the family since 1731, and is the only farm known to me, in that section of country, which was taken up and patented to the same family who still occupy it. On this farm, June 30, 1863, was fought the sharpest part of the cavalry skirmish before alluded to, or as the Comte de Paris calls it, the "Battle of Hanover," between the Union cavalry commanded by Kilpatrick and Custer, and the Confederates under Stuart. A Union soldier captured a Confederate flag in the field beyond the house, and received a medal from Congress for his gallantry. A Confederate soldier was carried, mortally wounded, into the sitting room and died there. The Confederates killed in the engagement were buried on the farm, where they fell; but most of the bodies were afterwards removed by friends.

Karle Forney was married to Mary Hay, of York, a descendant, through her mother, of the same Smyser family with which the Reistertown branch of the Forneys intermarried. They had six children: Samuel Hay, William Granville, Susan, John Wogan, Robert Lee, and George Franklin. The sons, with the exception of the eldest, have left Hanover—William and George living in Saratoga, Wyoming; Robert in Oakland, California, and John, who is a jeweler, in Steubenville, Ohio. The only daughter, Sue, who was the wife of Andrew Dellone, is dead.

Chapter VIII.

———

DESCENDANTS OF

DAVID FORNEY, PETER FORNEY, HANNAH (FORNEY) LA MOTTE AND
JACOB FORNEY, CHILDREN OF PHILIP FORNEY, AND GRAND
CHILDREN OF JOHANN ADAM FORNEY.

JOHANN ADAM FORNEY AND ELISABETHA LOWISA —.

PHILIP AND ELISABETH (SHERZ) FORNEY.

DAVID FORNEY, born November 7, 1763, died March 6, 1826, married LOUISA NACE, born 1772, died November 15, 1849.

Elizabeth, born April 26, 1792, died March 6, 1825.

Louisa, born October 20, 1794, died October 20, 1812.

MATTHIAS NACE, born September 4, 1796, died March 25, 1837, married May 12, 1827, AMANDA NACE, born September 6, 1803, died November 7, 1851.

Catharine Nace, born November 10, 1828, married December 23, 1851, Joseph Daugher Bittinger, born March 30, 1823, died April 14, 1885.

Lucy Forney.

Louisa Elizabeth, born June 9, 1830, married Oct. 26, 1851, Henry Wirt.

Anna Maria, born November 1, 1831.

George Nace, born February 25, 1833, married Oct. 19, 1858, Eliza A. Wirt.

Jacob Wirt, died November 3, 1885, married July 10, 1881, Ida Rebecca Oglesby.

Netta Amanda, married May 31, 1887, Ira W. Arnold.

Louise Forney, born February 5, 1889.

Matthias Nace, born March 23, 1835.

David Peter, born February 14, 1837, married May 17, 1861, Amanda Elizabeth Hinkle.

Carrie Emma, died March 9, 1867.
Anna Amanda.
George Matthias.
Henry Hinkle.
Louisa Elizabeth.
Catharine Eliza.
Margaret Rebecca.
Philip Nace.

Susan, born 1800, died September 17, 1821.

ANNA MARIA, married ROBERT BEVERIDGE.

Susan Louisa, born July 21, 1821, died May 31, 1850, married Jeremiah Fisher.

Alma Louisa, died December 29, 1876, married Henry Sage Manning.

Edith (died in infancy).
Richard Fisher.

Ella Beveridge, born November 19, 1851, died December 24, 1851.

Jeannette Beveridge, born March 21, 1854, died January 2, 1855.

Leila Beveridge, married William C. Howard.

Helen Louise, born January 31, 1878.
Margaret Merrill, born July 22, 1880, (died in infancy).
Ruth, born April 24, 1885.
William Fisher, born December 11, 1887.

Anna Eliza, born June 13, 1851, died July 1, 1879, married April 2, 1873, Cameron Haight King.

George Cameron, born Jan. 14, 1874.
Montrose Lochiel, born Aug. 25, 1875.
Cameron Haight, Jr., born July 4, 1877.

David Forney, born Nov. 6, 1852, married Nov. 24 1880, Addie King.

Walter Trembley, born Sept. 29, 1882.
David Forney, Jr., born Feb. 21, 1884.

George Fisher, born November 6, 1854.

David Forney, born 1827, died April 16, 1872, married August 6, 1850, Hannah Rebecca Winn, born 1828, died August 9, 1873.

Louisa Forney, born Nov. 6, 1856, married Dec. 14, 1876, Thomas Samuel Barton.

Ralph Clark, born October 25, 1881.

William Tiffany, born Jan. 18, 1857, married Nov. 9, 1887, Adolls Meachem.

Leland Stanford, born July 13, 1888.
William Meachem, born June 21, 1892.

Joseph Winn, born December 20, 1861, married November 26, 1890, Fannie Angeline Bullock.

Harry Hurlburt, born March 18, 1863.

Susan Caroline, born April 24, 1865, married Dec. 5, 1891, Harry Young.

Harry Beveridge, born June 20, 1893.

Mary Jeannette, born October 24, 1867, died October 11, 1873.

Robert Duval, born 1828, died 1836.

David, (died in childhood).

PETER FORNEY, born October 20, 1765, died April 29, 1840.

HANNAH FORNEY, born March 27, 1767, died 1794 (?), married JOHN HENRY LA MOTTE, died 1794 (?).

John (no records).

JACOB FORNEY, born October 12, 1770, died October 5, 1796 (?).

49

DAVID FORNEY married Louisa, daughter of Matthias and Elizabeth (Bowman) Nace; the Nace family had resided in Hanover since 1765, when Richard McAllister, the founder of Hanover, sold several of his town lots to "George Neas, tanner, of Baltimore town, in the Province of Maryland," probably the father of Matthias. Louisa Nace, however, was born near Taneytown, Md., and *her* father must have emigrated to Hanover. The Nace tannery, on Chestnut street, was a long-familiar landmark, and the "Nace Spring" is still so called in remembrance of the family who, for three generations, carried on the business of tanning there. David Forney and his wife, Lovis, as she sometimes wrote her name (her old friends called her Lovey Forney), removed to Baltimore, about 1791, and always resided there; he owned land on both sides of Fayette street, from Green to Fremont, and extending on the one side to Raborg street; his tannery stood at the corner of Fayette street and what is now Run alley. When the British attacked Baltimore, in 1814, David Forney and his son, Matthias, worked on the entrenchments to protect the city. His wife used often to recall the terrible British cannonade, which, unknown to her, was inspiring the song of "The Star Spangled Banner," and would say to her grandchildren, "Oh, children, I hope you will never hear such a dreadful sound," but those grandchildren were destined to listen to the three days' thunder of the guns of Gettysburg. David Forney was a very handsome man: he had a delicate constitution and died young.

The children of David and Louisa (Nace) Forney were Elizabeth Nace, Louisa (who died young), Matthias Nace, Susan, Anna Maria and David (who died young).

ELIZABETH NACE FORNEY died on the day of her father's death, in her thirty-fourth year.

MATTHIAS NACE FORNEY is thus described by his friend, Mr. George Frysinger, the founder of the *Hanover Herald:* "He was a native of Baltimore, and was well known in that city as an energetic young man, of more than ordinary talent, who could perform the arduous duty of a volunteer fireman or take his part in any enterprise gotten up. He had a strong predilection for the stage, and probably but for the influence of his mother and friends, would have followed that profession. After his marriage, he led a quiet life at the old residence (in Hanover), yet his active mind was ever devising something for the benefit of those around him. Among other things, he organized a dramatic association. A room was secured, a stage erected, scenery painted (mostly by Mr. F.), and a curtain fitted up. Several performances were given, to crowded audiences, but *the* piece was the production of "The Merchant of Venice," in which Mr. Forney took the part of Shylock. In after years I saw that character taken by star performers on the regular stage, but I never could divest myself of the opinion that Mr. Forney delineated the wily Jew as true to nature as the best of them. That fell disease, consumption, often laid him low, but he never flagged nor gave way to complaint. Early in 1835 he was engaged in demonstrating to men of means and money-lenders that a savings institution would be beneficial to the public and profitable to the stockholders. * * * Having taught F. E. Metzger the necessary book-keeping, and so forth, he resigned his position as treasurer, charged next to nothing for his services, and Mr. Metzger was appointed treasurer. Mr. Forney's health was very precarious, one day down and the next unexpectedly appearing up town, first visiting the institution and then the *Herald* office. As few of that day could comprehend a public spirited man like him, many could not bring themselves to believe that he had not some ulterior view of realizing money advantages; he asked the directors to appoint a committee to investigate the condition of the society. * * * The committee concluded that the institution had been well conducted, and that the officers had acted with good faith, etc. This settled the matter, and from that time on all cavil ceased. The society weathered the financial storm which followed the total downfall of the United States Bank, continued to declare regular as well as large extra dividends, took a first rank among similar institutions, and to-day its stock sells at treble its par value. Mr. Forney was an able writer, and took much interest in establishing the *Herald*. With the first number he commenced a series of piquant communications under the cognomen of "Ichabod Idle," only interrupted when he could not wield a pen. I received his last effusion in his room, which he must have written between his spells of coughing. It was as usual tinctured with humor, and bore no evidence that it was the production of a man who expected to breathe his last at any hour. It is almost needless to say that over a signature then well-known, I paid a last tribute to the memory of a noble man, and that the entire community concurred in all I said." He married Amanda, only child of George and Anna Catharine (Slagle) Nace. George Nace was a brother of Mrs. David Forney; he was an accomplished man—had traveled in Europe when that was a rare experience, had sat two years in the state legislature, was the first burgess of Hanover and one of its first postmasters, holding the office on the ground that he received more mail than any one else in the town; he also carried on the Nace tanyard. His wife, the daughter of Henry and Dorothy Slagle, was a woman of great force of character and sound good sense. Colonel Slagle was a prominent man, first "one of His Majesty's Justices of the Peace," and subsequently among the most active in resistance to that same "Majesty," He was Lieutenant-Colonel and afterwards Colonel of a batallion of Revolutionary militia in service during the winter of Valley Forge: was a member of the Committee of Correspondence for York County, held other offices under the Continental Congress, sat in two Constitutional Conventions and was appointed, in 1791, Associate Judge. He is described as "an ardent patriot, faithful officer and upright citizen."

The children of Matthias Nace and Amanda (Nace) Forney are Catharine Nace, Louisa Elizabeth, Anna Maria, George Nace, Matthias Nace and David Peter.

CATHARINE NACE FORNEY married the Rev. Joseph Baugher Bittinger, D. D. He was for a short time professor of Rhetoric in Middlebury College, in Vermont; then the first pastor of the Euclid Street Presbyterian Church in Cleveland, and afterwards for twenty years the faithful and beloved pastor of the Presbyterian Church at Sewickley, Pennsylvania. He wrote much and well, was a polished and forceful speaker, and interested in various reforms—notably in the Abolition movement and in prison reform. He was twice commissioned as the representative of his State in the Prison Congresses of London and Stockholm, and read papers at both meetings. His widow and one daughter, Lucy, reside in Sewickley.

LOUISA ELIZABETH FORNEY married Henry Wirt of Hanover. An account of him will be found among the descendants of Eva (Gelwicks) Wirt. Henry Wirt had no children.

ANNA MARIA FORNEY is unmarried and resides, most of the time, with her sister, Mrs. Wirt.

GEORGE NACE FORNEY is married to Eliza, daughter of Jacob and Amelia (Danner) Wirt. They have had two children—Jacob Wirt and Netta Amanda. Wirt graduated at Franklin and Marshall college, went to Colorado in search of health, but returning to Hanover, died there, in his 27th year. His widow (nee Ida Rebecca Oglesby, of Middletown, O.), is now re-married: he left no child. Netta is married to Ira W. Arnold, of Lancaster: they have one child, Louise Forney.

MATTHIAS NACE FORNEY entered in 1852, the shops of Ross Winans in Baltimore as an apprentice. Winans was then engaged in building locomotive engines for the Baltimore and Ohio road. After some years spent in the service of the Baltimore and Ohio Railroad and in mercantile business in Baltimore, he accepted a position in the machinery department of the Illinois Central Railroad, and spent the next few years in Chicago, afterwards removing to Boston to superintend the construction of some locomotives for the line. In some autobiographical notes furnished me, he says: "While employed with the Illinois Central Railroad Company, I designed an 'improved tank locomotive,' and applied for a patent on the invention. This kind of engine did not come into anything more than experimental use until ten years afterwards, when it was adopted on the New York Elevated Railroads. Since then no other kind of locomotive has been employed on those roads, and it has also been exclusively used on the Brooklyn and Chicago Elevated roads, and many were built for other roads. It is now a very popular form of engine for suburban and some other kinds of traffic. After the patent expired it was very generally adopted. In the fall of 1870 I accepted the position of associate editor of the *Railroad Gazette*, then published in Chicago. After the great fire the publication office of the paper was removed to New York. Soon after Mr. Dunning, who was the editor-in-chief, and myself bought the paper. In 1873 Mr. Dunning obtained a copy of a German book entitled, 'Katechismus der Einrichtung und des Betriebes der Locomotive," by George Kosak. We proposed to translate the book and adapt the translation to American practice in locomotive engineering. Before this plan was entertained, I had commenced an elementary treatise on the locomotive. In revising the translation of Mr. Kosak's book, it was found that the latter occupied only to a very limited extent the ground which I had 'staked out' in my own incomplete plan. The original intention was therefore abandoned, and the whole book was rewritten. It was first published in the *Railroad Gazette*, and afterwards in book form with the title of the 'Catechism of the Locomotive.' It met with great favor. In 1889 it was thoroughly revised, made nearly double its original size, and a new edition issued. Up to the present time, the book has had a large sale. The following quotation from the preface of the 'Car Builders' Dictionary,' will help to explain my agency in the preparation of that book: 'Ever since the general interchange of cars among different railroads, a great deal of inconvenience, confusion and delay has been caused to those who build and repair them by the want of common names for the different parts of cars. One part is known by one name at one place, and by quite different names at other places: and, what causes still worse confusion, a term often means one thing on one road and quite a different thing on another. The art of car building, in fact, has grown more rapidly than the language relating to it. Early in the history of the Master Car Builders' Association this subject attracted attention, and, in 1871 a committee was appointed to prepare a Dictionary of Terms used in Car building. This committee was finally narrowed down to Messrs. Leander Garey, Calvin A. Smith and myself, who were courageous enough to undertake the task of completing the work, probably, only because they were then quite ignorant of its magnitude. Altogether it was one of the most difficult and laborious pieces of work I ever undertook, and absorbed an immense amount of labor. The whole plan and arrangement of the book was novel, as will be seen by referring to it. How alluring, and it may perhaps be said, deceptive, the foible of invention is, the following list of my patents will show. I have taken out five patents on locomotives, six on car seats, and one each on furnace-doors, car bodies, safe depositories for cars, a fire-grate and steam boilers. The patents on car seats are beginning to be profitable, the others have afforded me much diversion, but thus far little money. I continued to publish the *Railroad Gazette* until 1883 when my health demanded rest from incessant editorial work. In the latter part of that year I sold my interest in the paper, and gave up active business. For three years—my life seems to have been divided into cycles of three years—I was not engaged in any regular business. Doing nothing soon grew wearisome, and in the latter part of 1886, for the sake of having regular occupation, I bought the *American Railroad Journal* and *Von Nostrand's Engineering Magazine*, and consolidated the two publications under the name of the *American Engineer and Railroad Journal*.

DAVID PETER FORNEY is a farmer, residing in Adams county, near Hanover, and has taken an active part in addressing farmers' conventions of various kinds, having been appointed by the governor of Pennsylvania a delegate to several such bodies. He has also written considerably for agricultural papers. He is married to Amanda, daughter of George W. Hinkle, M. D., and his second wife, Anna Harnish; they have had eight children—Carrie Emma (who died in infancy), Anna Amanda, George Matthias, Henry Hinkle, Louisa Elizabeth, Catharine Eliza, Margaret Rebecca and Philip Nace.

SUSAN FORNEY, daughter of David and Louisa Forney, died young of consumption. In the last stages of her illness, she became restless and thought she would be better at her brother Matthias' home in Hanover; she was taken thither, but sank under the fatigues of the forty-mile ride and died in a few days; she is buried in the old Reformed graveyard there.

ANNA MARIA FORNEY is said to have been a beautiful woman—"the most fairy-like person I ever saw," says an old friend. She married Robert Beveridge, a Scotchman; with him she went to Florida, then a wilderness, where the Indians terrified her by coming to her door to beg. There her husband and a business partner laid out a town, which they named in honor of their wives—Mary and Anna—transformed into "Marianna," where Mrs. Beveridge died, and is buried. The children of Robert and Anna Maria (Forney) Beveridge were Susan Louisa, David Forney and Robert Duval. The last named, who died in childhood, owed his middle name to the fact that Governor Duval of Florida, was staying in the house when he was born.

SUSAN LOUISA BEVERIDGE was brought up by her grandmother, who took her daughter's children to her home in Baltimore, after their mother's death. She married Jeremiah Fisher, then a merchant in Baltimore. Two of their children, Jeannette and

Ella, died in childhood, within a few days of each other. Mrs. Fisher's health failed after this, and after a vain attempt to regain strength by a visit to Florida, among her father's family by his second marriage, she returned to Baltimore to die. Mr. Fisher lost his property, his health became greatly impaired and a few years after, he was found dead in Druid Hill Park. The children of Jeremiah and Susan (Beveridge) Fisher were Anna Louisa, Jeannette Beveridge, Ella Beveridge and Leila Beveridge.

LOUISE FISHER, with her sister Leila, was brought up after her parents' death by a friend of the family, Mrs. Merrill, of Portland, Me. She was a strikingly beautiful person. She married Henry Sage Manning, of Brooklyn, and died young, leaving a son, Richard; her little daughter, Edith, who died before her mother, is the baby—

> "A dream of sunshine, and all that's sweet,
> Of all that is pure and bright;
> Of eyes that were blue as the sky by day,
> And as soft as the stars by night."—

alluded to in the Rev. John Chadwick's poems of "Three Happy Souls" and "The Two Waitings."

LEILA BEVERIDGE FISHER is married to William C. Howard, of Brooklyn, and has had four children—Helen Louise, Margaret Merrill (who died in infancy), Ruth and William Fisher.

DAVID FORNEY BEVERIDGE went to California in the early days of the gold fever; there he lost his right arm by an accident while hunting; he returned with his family to Baltimore, but subsequently went back to California, where he died. He married Hannah Rebecca Winn, who belonged to a Salem (Mass.) family. They had nine children; Anna Eliza, David Forney, George Fisher, Louisa Forney, William Tiffany, Joseph Winn, Harry Hurlbert, Susan Caroline and Mary Jeannette, who died in childhood.

ANNA ELIZA BEVERIDGE was married to Cameron H. King, a lawyer, of Oakland, California, where she died, leaving three sons.

DAVID FORNEY BEVERIDGE, JR., resides in Vallejo, California, is a pattern maker by occupation, and has two sons.

GEORGE FISHER BEVERIDGE is a mining engineer in Portland, Oregon.

LOUISA FORNEY BEVERIDGE, to whose painstaking collection I owe these facts concerning her family, is married to T. S. Barton of San Francisco, and has one child.

WILLIAM TIFFANY BEVERIDGE, a county surveyor, is married to Adelis Meachem, and has, like the others of the family, no daughters, but two sons.

JOSEPH WINN BEVERIDGE is foreman of the Lewis & Dryden Printing Company, of Portland, Oregon.

HARRY HURLBERT BEVERIDGE is farming at Banning, California.

SUSAN CAROLINE BEVERIDGE, married to Harry Young, resides in San Francisco.

PETER FORNEY, son of Philip, lived in Baltimore all his adult life, engaged with his brother Jacob in the wholesale grocery business; he died unmarried. His will, in which he left bequests to many relatives, has been a fruitful source of family history; he also provided for the building of a burial vault, in which most of the family who had lived in Baltimore were interred, until the city put a street through the burial ground and the remains were removed to Hanover.

54

HANNAH FORNEY is said by Mr. Daniel Lammot to have married John Henry La-Motte, a brother of Elizabeth Forney's husband. They lived in Baltimore; there her husband died and she soon followed him, dying, it is said, of a broken heart. They had but one son, John, who left Baltimore about 1810, going either to Mississippi or Missouri, where he was lost sight of.

JACOB FORNEY died young, in Baltimore, on the day on which he was to have been married to "a very lovely young woman, Catharine Myers;" he was buried in his wedding suit. He seems to have been much beloved in his family; several persons, including Jacob Forney, of Hanover, son of Adam, were named for him.

Chapter IX.

———

DESCENDANTS OF

SUSANNA (FORNEY) DECKER AND SALOME (FORNEY) GROVE. DAUGH-
TERS OF PHILIP FORNEY, AND GRAND CHILDREN
OF JOHANN ADAM FORNEY.

JOHANN ADAM FORNEY AND ELISABETHA LOWISA ——.

PHILIP AND ELISABETH (SHERZ) FORNEY.

JACOB FORNEY, born 1794, married JULIA HERRING.
- George.
- Louis.

SUSANNA FORNEY, born October 5, 1775, died January 3, 1854, married 1793, GEO. DECKER, died November 26, 1846.

SALOME, born May 26, 1796, died November 9, 1882, married October 22, 1818, MICHAEL DIFFENDERFFER, born May 11, 1790, died September 17, 1870.

- Susan Christian, born September 2, 1819.
- George Michael, born April 1, 1821, died May 17, 1822.
- William Henry, born February 1, 1822, married November 8, 1858, Rebecca B. Kelso.
  - Nellie, born September 16, 1859, died February 27, 1861.
  - Salome Decker, born 1860, died 1865.
  - William D., born 1861.
  - John Kingsbury Elgee, born 1863.
  - George Young Kelso, born July 8, 1867, married May 11, 1892, Eliza Grolella Groverman.
  - Clarence Rich, born October 20, 1868.
- George Decker, born May 20, 1823, died July 8, 1825.
- Louis Albers, born October 22, 1826, died June 15, 1861, married Christina Dick.
  - Louis Albers, born February 2, 1861.
- Michael Addison, born July 31, 1828, died May 21, 1829.
- Lydia Louise, born February 13, 1829, died July 30, 1830.
- Salome, born April 3, 1832, married September 16, 1861, Montgomery Johns.
  - Nannie Montgomery, born July, 1862, married January 17, 1882, Horace Slingluff.
    - Horace.
    - Judith.
    - Margaret.
    - Montgomery.
    - Annette.
  - Salome Lavinia, born November, 1863, married September 16, 1879, Daniel C. Hopper.
    - Mary Johns.
    - Salome Lavinia.
    - Annie.
    - Ayletta.
  - Henry Van Dyke, married —— Harden.
- Sophia Catharine, born January 7, 1834, died June, 1834.
- Georgiana Decker, born February 1, 1835.
- Michael, born August 30, 1838, married June 2, 1869, Rebecca Talbot.
  - Honora McKenzie.
  - John Talbot.
  - Bessie.
  - (died 1878.)
- Harrison, born August 26, 1840, married November 23, 1886, Mary Rosalie Bailey.
  - Salome.
  - Mary Rosalie.
  - Henry Harrison.
  - Susan.
  - Clarence.
  - Malcolm.

LYDIA, born 1798, died 1843.

ELIZABETH MARGARETTA, born August 17, 1800, died March 28, 1861.

SALOME FORNEY, born February 20, 1776, died April 22, 1859, married March 12, 1807, STEPHEN GROVE, born October 25, 1776, died November 20, 1848.

CATHARINE SUSANNA, born October 11, 1811, married November 29, 1832, OTIS SPEAR, born August 20, 1802, died October 31, 1875.

- Sarah Lydia, born September 9, 1833, married November 29, 1850, Samuel H. Giesy.
  - Otis (died in infancy).
  - Herbert.
- James Otis, born June 18, 1835, married October 22, 1868, Elizabeth Davis Law.
  - Margaretta.
  - Catharine.
  - Louisa.
  - James.
- Alvah Grove, born August 26, 1837, died August 30, 1865.
- Peter Forney, born September 27, 1839, married October 22, 1863, Anna Heagy.
  - Elizabeth Grove.
  - Elsie Elliott, died February 19, 1893.
- Harrison, born January 23, 1841, died September 18, 1874.
- Edwin Walker, born November 23, 1845, married Emaline Fuller.
  - Amanda Catharine.
  - William Otis.
- Enoch Pratt, born November 28, 1847.
- Anna Harrison (died in infancy).

JACOB FORNEY, born April 2, 1813, married April 27, 1845, MARGARETTA RAMSAY.
- Salome Forney, married Mardoch Howell.
- Allen, married John McCoy.
- Anna, married Charles Felton.
- Kate, married Henry Register.

57

Susanna Forney was married to George Decker, a revolutionary soldier, who entered mercantile life in Baltimore about 1786. They had three children—Jacob Forney, Salome and Lydia.

Jacob Forney Decker was all his life in the Commercial and Farmers Bank of Baltimore; he was a member of the association of the "Old Defenders," who had served in the battle of North Point. He married, rather late in life, Julia Herring, and they had two sons, George and Louis, of whom I have no information.

Salome Decker married Dr. Michael Diffenderffer, who was a surgeon in the war of 1812, and was engaged in the battle of North Point; he was at the time of his death the oldest practicing physician in Baltimore, living in the same house for fifty-eight years. Michael and Salome (Decker) Diffenderffer had twelve children—Susan Christina, George Michael, William Henry, George Decker, Louis Albers, Michael Addison, Lydia Louise, Salome, Sophia Catharine, Georgiana Decker, Michael and Henry Harrison. Five of these children died in their infancy; the survivors were Susan, William, Louis, Salome, Georgiana, Michael and Harry.

Susan Diffenderffer lives in Baltimore, and it is to her kindness that I am indebted for all the information concerning this branch of the family.

William Diffenderffer is a practicing physician in Baltimore and an active member of the Episcopal church. He and his wife (*nee* Rebecca Kelso), have had six children—Nellie, Salome Decker, William D., John Kingsbury Elgee, George Young Kelso, and Clarence Rich. Both daughters died in childhood, the younger at sea, of yellow fever.

Louis Diffenderffer resided in Louisville, Ky., where he married Christina Dick, and, dying there, left one son who bears the same name as his father.

Salome Diffenderffer lives in Baltimore; she was married to Montgomery Johns, a son of the Rev. Dr. Johns, an Episcopal clergyman well known there in former times; she has three children—Nannie Montgomery, married to Horace Slingluff; Salome Lavinia, the wife of Daniel C. Hopper, and Henry Van Dyke, married to Miss Harden.

Georgiana Diffenderffer lives with her eldest sister in Baltimore and has long been engaged in teaching.

Michael Diffenderffer is married to Rebecca Talbot; they have had three children, who died within a few days of each other, of scarlet fever.

Harrison Diffenderffer resided in Ohio when the Civil War broke out, and entering a regiment from that state, served throughout the war. He is married to Mary Rosalie Bailey and they have six children.

Lydia Decker died, unmarried, in Baltimore.

SALOME FORNEY was commonly called "Sally," and her name has been given as Sarah; but she herself signed it as I have given it. She married Stephen Grove, like herself a native of York county, but after their marriage they lived on Green street, Baltimore, near David Forney's home. She was early left a widow with three children—Elizabeth Margaretta, Catharine Susanna and Jacob Forney.

ELIZABETH MARGARETTA GROVE died, unmarried, in Baltimore.

CATHARINE SUSANNA GROVE was married to Otis Spear, a native of Ludlow, Vt., but who long resided in Baltimore. Mr. Spear is now dead but his widow survives him, and it is to her that I am indebted for most of the facts regarding the younger children of Philip Forney, which are embodied in these later chapters. Otis and Catharine (Grove) Spear had eight children—Sarah Lydia, James Otis, Alvah Grove, Peter Forney, Edwin Walker, Harrison, Enoch Pratt, and Anna Harrison, who died in infancy.

SARAH LYDIA SPEAR married the Rev. Samuel H. Giesy, D. D,, a clergyman who died as the pastor of the (Episcopal) Church of the Epiphany in Washington, D. C. His widow, with one son, Herbert, a member of the bar, still resides in the Capital.

OTIS SPEAR lives in Baltimore, and is married to Elizabeth, daughter of Major Law, at one time mayor of the city; they have four children.

ALVAH SPEAR carred on a large paper mill in Mobile; he was killed by an explosion on board the steamer Reindeer while on his way home, after an absence of seven years.

FORNEY and EDWIN SPEAR reside in Baltimore; both are married and have families.

HARRY SPEAR entered the U. S. Navy during the Civil War; afterward he was assistant engineer on the flag-ship "Hartford," in the East India squadron, and on the "Saranac." His health failed, and he died of consumption, after a long illness, in Baltimore. He was unmarried.

PRATT SPEAR, who holds the place of clerk at the Mt. Vernon hotel in Baltimore, is named in honor of Enoch Pratt, the venerable philanthropist of Baltimore, who was an early friend and business associate of his father.

JACOB FORNEY GROVE also lived in Baltimore, and was married to Margaretta Ramsay, the daughter of a ship-captain living in that part of the city known as the "Old Town." Jacob Forney and Margaretta (Ramsay) Grove had four daughters—Salome Forney, Alice, Anna and Kate. Salome is married to Murdoch Howell; they have six children. Alice is married to the Rev. John McCoy, D. D., and has one child; Anna, to Mr. Felton; she has three children; Kate is married to Henry Register, and they have two children.